I Have Issues
Mom & Dad
Thought Provoking Parenting Stories

Dr Bindu Selot

STERLING PAPERBACKS
An imprint of
Sterling Publishers (P) Ltd.
Regd. Office: A-59, Okhla Industrial Area, Phase-II,
New Delhi-110020. CIN: U22110PB1964PTC002569
Tel: 26387070, 26386209; Fax: 91-11-26383788
E-mail: mail@sterlingpublishers.com
www.sterlingpublishers.com

I Have Issues, Mom and Dad
Thought Provoking Parenting Stories
© 2015, Dr Bindu Selot
ISBN 978 81 207 9655 3

All rights are reserved.
No part of this publication may be reproduced, stored in a retrieval system or transmitted, in any form or by any means, mechanical, photocopying, recording or otherwise, without prior written permission of the author.

Printed in India
Printed and Published by Sterling Publishers Pvt. Ltd.,
New Delhi-110020.

Dedication

I dedicate this book to my parents
Col. K. N Mishra and Mrs Mamta Mishra

My Mom and Dad have been my first and the most impactful teachers. They have been my source of inspiration and constant strength in every walk of my life. My parents have been my role models. It was through their unconditional love, faith, and belief that I could evolve and reach where I am today.

My Mom taught me compassion, resilience, unconditional love, commitment, and how to always look at the positives in every situation and in every human being. My Dad taught me leadership, responsibility, humility, never-say-die attitude, and how to always be open to learning from each and every situation. Above all, my parents taught me to be happy, to always live in the present moment, and take life as it comes. They taught me how to make a difference in other people's lives.

Thank you, God, for blessing me with the most invaluable gift—my parents! Love you Mom and Dad.

Acknowledgements

First of all, I would like to thank you, God, for blessing me each time I gathered myself to write this book. Thank you Mom, Dad, and my Brother for always being my strength.

I take pride in extending my heartfelt thanks to my husband, Rajeev Selot, who inspired me to write this second book of mine. Immediately after the launch of my first book in February 2014, Rajeev said, "Hey, one book can happen by chance. But if you are an author in the true sense, then you must start working on your next book from now." It was because of this thought in my subconscious mind that I could produce this second book.

My sincere thanks to Ms Sapna Chauhan, Vice Chairperson Amiown (Amity's Caring Preschools) and ACERT (Amity Center for Educational Research and Training), to have given me the wonderful opportunity of being actively involved in the process of teaching and learning, which nourishes my mind and helps in creativity and divergent thinking. I want to extend my special thanks to all the respected members of the Amity Management who have wholeheartedly validated my work and have motivated me always, as a result of which I could meaningfully contribute to the process of change.

My special thanks to all the people that I have interacted with in my personal and professional life, my friends, and my family, who have inspired me to write these thought provoking stories.

I extend my sincere gratitude to Mr S. K. Ghai, Managing Director, Sterling Publishers Pvt. Ltd., for believing in my second book proposal and also giving me an opportunity to work with Mr Sanjiv Sarin, the editor or my previous book, once again. Mr Ghai's enthusiasm and energy is infectious. Every time I interacted with him, I felt motivated and energetic. A special thanks to his staff for all their efforts in the making of this book.

I want to specially thank my editor, Mr Sanjiv Sarin, for being so encouraging during the process of editing. His keen eye for every detail and immense patience ensured an amazing final product that you are holding in your hands.

I extend my heartfelt thanks to the entire team of ACERT and Amiown, all my students at ACERT, and all my Amiown teachers who have, lovingly, been motivating me during my journey as an author.

Last, but not the least, I extend my thanks, with love, to my two sons, Chirag and Roshan, who have evolved to be responsible, independent young adults, who made sure that I had enough time on my hands to invest in my dream and who contributed to giving the titles to the stories and the book. It is a blessing to interact with them always, even now when they are 20 and 17 years old. We, as a family, end up talking for hours and hours, and we all lose the track of the time. This bond of communication and togetherness is the backbone of our relationship and we, as parents, cherish every moment of it.

Nothing can ever be complete without my bundle of unconditional love, my pet dog Maddy. Thank you, Maddy, for always cuddling in my lap during this unique journey of mine and silently contributing in a big way in the making of this book.

Thank you, God, for blessing me with such a supportive family, my sense of purpose in this life, and such a wonderful workplace. It is because of these blessings that I am able to contribute in my humble way to make a difference to the society I live in.

Preface

In this book, *I Have Issues, Mom and Dad*. I have tried to explore some of the major issues that children have because of the parenting practices of their Moms and Dads. I have, through a collection of 11 stories, tried to look for some thoughtful and practical solutions to address these issues of parenting. I firmly believe that, with the reflective practices mentioned towards the end of the stories, we will be able to find workable solutions to these issues and make the parent-child relationship a real strong one because "The family is the first line of defence, especially for children and a major factor in their survival, health, education, development, and protection. It is also a major source of nurturance, emotional bonding, and socialization and a link between continuity and change" (Sonawat, 2001).

Parenting, my dear friends, is a life-long journey. As I have experienced a part of it and continue to experience it now as well, it is a journey of evolution and change. Since our children are an integral part of an ever-changing environment, there will be issues as a result of the generation gap. The only mantra for parenting today is to resolve these issues as quickly as possible. This can only be achieved by removing our age old biases and preconceived notions and by getting down to the level of our children to understand them and, in turn, grow together with them.

By virtue of being a practicing Parent Counsellor and officially being associated with Amiown (Amity's Caring Preschools) and ACERT, (Amity Center for Educational Research and Training), I meet many parents who discuss their concerns with me. I also get many opportunities to interact with children, who share their feelings openly with me.

As a result of this amazing journey, and personally as a parent, I have gathered a lot of experience of other parents, children, and their individual journeys.

Many parents, on reflection, found that life would have been different only if they had understood parenting and had taken different decisions. I, somehow, wanted to reach a larger audience of parents to share what I had learned so far, with the idea that I may be able to make that little, but crucial, difference in some child's life. So this book, which you are holding in your hands, came about.

Unknowingly, through our individual parenting practices, we are constantly contributing in the character formation of our children. This has been well depicted in my stories. It is, therefore, our moral responsibility to become aware and fine-tune our parenting approaches to suit the emotional, mental, and physical development needs of our children. I find today's parents very conscious, open, and eager to know what they could have done better to make a difference in the lives of their children.

With these thoughts, I decided to keep the format of the book in a story form, because human brains have been wired to listen to stories. In fact, I prefer to begin my sessions with a story and, like I always do after a story, I have tried to explore the issues of parenting through reflections and then attempted to look for some workable strategies.

These are all real-life stories that I have gathered from my environment, that is, my family, friends, relatives, or clients, who are parents, as well as from children.

I am sure that anybody who reads this book will connect with the content without even coming to know of it, because my stories are a reflection of the society which we are an integral part of. And I also am sure that everyone's takeaway from the stories would be different, unique, and their very own.

All our children are born pure and precious. It is the experiences and environment they get nurtured in that is responsible for individual differences and contributes to the personalities they become. It is never too late, dear Parents. We can't change the past, but let's begin from today, let's contribute consciously to the task of parenting, and take those tiny steps required to make this journey of parenting a meaningful one, because our children are our most prized possessions.

Let us have faith and belief in our children, that they will become responsible, independent citizens of our society. Let us also be proud of our parenting practices and contribute in the metamorphosis of our children.

There are a number of books whose contents I found relevant to my thought process. I have shared the list in the bibliography. The bibliography has two purpose. The first is to thank all the writers whose books I have studied as a parent and as a Parent Counsellor. The second, of course, is to offer you a list of suggested readings for your parenting journey.

Wishing you an informed parenting journey!

Dr Bindu Selot

Contents

Acknowledgements   5
Preface   7

1. Whose Dream Was It?   11
2. Why Did You Make Me a Cripple?   23
3. PTM—Not Again!   33
4. Don't Send Me to a Coaching School   42
5. Why Don't You Listen to Me, Mom?   48
6. Can You Ever Understand Me?   56
7. Were You Ready for Me?   65
8. Do You Trust Me on Money Matters?   74
9. Stop Micromanaging My Life! Give Me a Break!   84
10. I Was Adopted! The Shocking Truth   92
11. I Got Carried Away   97

Bibliography   111

1

Whose Dream Was It?

Molly was a very sweet, pleasant girl who lived with her parents, a younger sister, and her grandmother. Her grandfather had died in a road accident before Molly was born. Life was good for Molly and her sister, though their grandmother was very strict with them and often compared them with the other children. But as long as her mother loved her and understood her, Molly was fine with the little odd behaviour of her grandmother.

Molly's mother was the Principal of a Senior Secondary School and her father was a doctor. Molly was more of an outdoor person—she loved sports and was always a good performer, which her grandmother did not like at all.

When Molly came to Class 9, her mother told her, "Molly, you just have a few more days in this school. I am now shifting you to my school, so that I can pay more attention to you and your studies. Class 9 and 10 are crucial classes because based on them, you will be given your stream." Molly was shocked and in tears. How could she leave her friends? What would happen to the matches that she had to play? She was an excellent basketball player and her team depended on her. How could she desert her team?

Molly's mother was stern in her response. "Molly, enough is enough! We have had enough of your sports. You cannot make a career in sports. Now it is time for you to get back to your studies and become serious in life. So better prepare yourself. I am not taking a 'No' from you!"

So Molly was shifted to her Mom's school, to a new class with new friends. She felt depressed and lonely, but slowly and gradually she started adjusting to the new environment that she was forced into by her mother. But she missed her old school, her friends, and teachers.

Within a short span of time, she became one of the favourites of the sports teacher. She was selected in the school team and made many friends as well. Everything seemed fine.

Then the first term exams began. Soon, the day for getting the report card also arrived. Molly, purposely, did not go to school that day because she knew that she would have barely passed somehow and her Mom would be very unhappy with her.

Molly's mother came late in the evening that day because, as a Principal, she had lot of meetings to attend. She called Molly and scolded her for the marks she had got. Molly had managed to get only 50 per cent overall. Molly's mother said to her, "I am ashamed of you. Can you imagine, I am the Principal of the school and my daughter, who should be a role model for all other students, has managed to pass with great difficulty?"

Molly was scared. She also felt guilty that she had let her Mom down. She promised to study hard and come first in the class in the next exam. She also confessed that she found a couple of subjects difficult and needed tuitions. Her mother readily agreed and arranged for them.

Molly started studying hard. Every day she had one tuition or the other. She kept her promise and came first not only in her section, but in all the sections of her class.

The rest of the Class 9 and 10 passed smoothly because Molly was always the topper. She scored a CGPA of 10 in her Class 10 boards. Her mother was very happy and proud of her daughter.

Though to everybody else everything seemed fine, but Molly was actually losing touch with her inner self. She had almost given up all the sports because they were a big waste of time according to her mother. She had great faith in her mother and accepted her advice that there was no other way except to quit sports and study hard to make your life.

Ultimately, the day came when they had to decide the stream to take in Class 11. Molly was very confused. She was still trying to figure out what she actually liked and wanted. So when her mother decided for her and announced that Molly had taken Science and would become a doctor like her Dad, Molly almost choked and could hardly speak. She, thus, became a Science student, with a combination of PCMB (Physics, Chemistry, Maths, and Biology).

In the first term exam in Class 11, Molly failed in almost all the subjects, except English. Her mother took all the responsibility of Molly's failure. She submitted her resignation, saying that her daughter was getting neglected because of her duties as a Principal. After resigning she would take charge of Molly's studies. She would teach her Biology and English. Physics, Chemistry, and Maths would be taught by other tutors.

The pressure on Molly increased. She stopped talking to her friends. She stopped going out with the family for dinners or movies because she felt she would be wasting her time. She also had to go to classes at the coaching institute on Saturdays and Sundays to prepare for medical entrance exams. Life for Molly was just books and tuitions.

Then discussions started to send her to a residential coaching centre so that she could focus all her time and attention on studies. Molly did not want to go at all, but by this time she had stopped sharing her true feelings with her parents. Because one of her friends was also going there, she agreed to go to the coaching centre to prepare for the entrance exams.

Barely a month later, Molly's parents had to rush to the centre because she had fainted in the class and had hurt herself badly. Molly was shown to a doctor, who prescribed few tests. When the reports came, it was found that her haemoglobin had gone down to 6. She was immediately rushed back to her home and hospitalized. She had to be given blood transfusion.

Finally, she recovered, felt better, and came home. At home, Molly's parents and grandmother had decided that she would not be sent away again. Instead, she would go back to her previous school.

Once again, routine life began for Molly. Between school, tuitions, coaching classes, and study sessions with her Mom, she had no time for anything else. Her Mom started micromanaging her life. Molly felt stifled.

Molly had to live by the clock. Every minute of hers was closely monitored so that not even a single second was wasted. It was as if the house had become a school, with just one student. The only discussion in the house was subjects, tuitions, boards, marks, medical colleges, and whose son or daughter got admitted where.

Finally, the D-Day arrived. The Class 12 board results were out. Molly had scored 72 per cent. She was quite happy and satisfied, because only she knew the price that she had paid to get this percentage. After all, what else can one expect when one has to mug up everything the way Molly had to? Molly had little interest in the subjects she had been forced to take. So she had to memorize everything, without understanding the topics.

As expected, Molly's mother was shocked. So was her grandmother. Only her Dad appeared unaffected. She was compared with the relatives and her friends. Molly's mother acted as if she was ashamed of her daughter.

Molly felt guilty. Once again she had failed in making her parents happy. But what could she do? She had done her best and more than this was impossible for her to achieve.

Another black day arrived when the medical entrance results were declared. Molly had not qualified for a single college, while two of her friends who had taken the same coaching had succeeded. Molly felt terrible. She thought she was useless. All her family members appeared shocked, too, and communicated their feelings to her.

Another major decision was taken by her Mom. Molly dropped one year and again started preparing for medical entrance exams. This time Molly seemed to be punishing herself—her smile had vanished, her life revolved around her coaching classes, tuitions from her mother, and self-study. She ate little, had no friends, hardly interacted with her family or friends, did not like meeting people, and most of the time locked herself in her room in the name of study and exam preparations.

A year passed. Once again it was time for the declaration of the results. And the most dreadful thing happened—Molly could not make it to any medical college at all.

In the meantime, her parents had started searching and exploring the options of getting her admitted in a private medical college. However, this was the last option. Molly's parents gathered information about the expenditure which would be incurred if she went to a private college. But after a lot of thinking and evaluation, they came to the conclusion that it was beyond their means.

By now Molly and her parents had become emotionally drained. In fact, Molly's haemoglobin level had gone down once again and was she was slipping into a state of depression. Her parents became extremely worried.

Molly was put on medication and the doctor told the parents that she was extremely stressed, depressed, and highly anxious. She had a very low self-opinion. He counselled them to make efforts to bring Molly back to normal life using the help of a professional counsellor.

As per the doctor's advice, Molly's parents visited a counsellor. They were shocked to know, after the first session which Molly had with the counsellor, that Molly had never wanted to become a doctor! Instead, she always dreamt of becoming a singer and she was missing her much-loved sports as well.

The first thing for Molly's parents was acceptance. This took some time for them. Once they accepted the facts, along with the counsellor, they worked towards exploring what could be done.

Molly has now joined a music college where she learns music. She has also become a member of a sports complex where she goes regularly for basketball coaching and swimming. She has enrolled in a college and is in the first year of B.Sc. Together with her family and the counsellor, Molly is still trying to figure out her options after graduation. Let's hope that she can, finally, make a profession out of her passion.

In the meantime she has come back to her normal self and has started enjoying life. There is huge load of guilt which Molly's Mom is carrying. Now she is the one who advises parents not to push their children to achieve their own unfulfilled dreams. Parents should simply expect their children to be healthy and happy.

But everyone is not so lucky. Let me share another story of a boy named Sanjay. He says, "In a bid to keep my Mom and Dad happy, I have ruined my life completely." This is how the story goes:

Sanjay was an outgoing, sweet little boy. He loved exploring his environment and could make friends easily. He lived with his Mom and Dad and his lovely sister and was happy with his life.

His Dad was an army officer and Mom was a teacher. So there was strict discipline in the house. Sanjay and his sister were scared of their father because he was a perfectionist and always wanted his children to be the same. Come what may, the whole house was up in the morning at 5 a.m. Nobody was allowed to sleep in the afternoon. There was a fixed time for all meals and table manners had to be strictly followed. Sanjay and his sister felt oppressed by the regulations and controls.

When their father was not around, their behaviour was completely different. They loved being themselves in his absence. Their mother was at peace with everything around, so she was not a challenge at all.

Sanjay and his sister were under constant pressure of coming first not only in the class but also in every activity they participated. Their Dad accepted only the best. Even if they came second in anything, words like "useless", "hopeless", and "fit for nothing" were hurled at them by him. The major brunt had to be borne by Sanjay, because he was elder.

Time passed and soon it was time to decide the stream that Sanjay would take after Class 10. No choices were permitted, because his Dad, from his childhood days, had impressed on him that he had to take Science with PCM group (Physics, Chemistry, Maths) and that he had to go for engineering in college, because that was the best thing for him. So Sanjay, without a second thought, opted for Science. He also registered for tuitions for entrance exams of engineering colleges.

So Monday to Friday was school. On Saturday and Sunday, for the whole day, he would be in the tuition centre, preparing for the engineering entrance exams. There was no time for socialization, friends, or any co-curricular activities. No outings, parties, or night outs were allowed to him, since the priority was studying and preparation for his future career.

In the meantime, Sanjay's sister had also reached Class 10. For her also, the career path had been made clear from her childhood days. Her army officer Dad had instilled in her that she needed to study medicine and become a doctor, because that was the best profession for girls.

So the journeys of an engineer and a doctor had begun. Sanjay came out with flying colours and topped his school. He qualified for the best engineering college. There was a festive mood in their house. Sanjay's Dad and Mom were getting all the congratulations for bringing up their children so well. There were compliments from the family, friends, and relatives. There were a series of parties to celebrate. Sanjay's Dad and Mom were very proud of themselves and the way they had made their son to focus to becoming an engineer.

Sanjay happily left his home for the engineering college and the final journey of four years of becoming an engineer had begun. In the meantime, Sanjay's sister also completed her school. She scored 90 per cent marks, but could not top the school. She qualified to study in a renowned medical college. She was on her way to becoming a doctor.

In the first semester break at the engineering college, Sanjay, on the pretext of studying and completing a project, stayed back in the college. In the second semester break also, Sanjay did not come home. When his Dad called him on phone, there was no response. For the first time, Sanjay did not pick up his Dad's phone. Sanjay stopped taking his Mom's calls as well.

His parents became worried. They called the college authorities. Through them they got a message from him that he was busy. This behaviour was not like Sanjay's, so his Mom asked her brother, Sanjay's maternal uncle, to talk to him and find out what was going on.

Sanjay's maternal uncle took leave and visited him in college. After that he went to Sanjay's parents and revealed what he had heard from Sanjay.

Sanjay said he would never go home, because he hated his Dad and Mom. He had never wanted to become an engineer. But his Dad never asked him what he wanted to do. He was like Hitler. His parents were always trying to achieve their unfulfilled dreams through him. There was a constant pressure on performance and he was supposed to come first in everything. He said that because of this pressure, he lost all his friends. He had no outings, no enjoyment, and no breaks—just study, perform, come first, then again study, compete, come first.

As a result of all this, Sanjay felt that he had become a loner. He knew nothing other than books. In spite of the fact that he came first and was in the best engineering college, he was not happy. And he threatened his parents that if they tried to put any kind of pressure on him, he would commit suicide.

Sanjay's parents were not just shocked—they were shattered. They could not believe what they were hearing. In spite of all the relatives, family, and friends trying to counsel Sanjay, he did not come back home. His parents thought that, maybe, with the passage of time things will improve.

When he was in the fourth year, one day, suddenly, Sanjay's parents got a call from the college that they needed to come and take Sanjay back home, because Sanjay had become addicted to drugs. This was a very sad news. Sanjay's parent's reached his college, packed his bags, and brought him home. He was sent to a deaddiction centre, counselled, and treated. Throughout all this, his parents were with him, very closely monitoring, caring, and supporting him.

Finally, Sanjay managed to come out of the clutches of drugs, went back to college after a year, has now completed his engineering degree, and is back home. But he is still trying to figure out what to do next because, unfortunately, he does not want to pick up any job in the field of engineering.

His sister was lucky. She finished her medical studies and now has her own clinic. She is very successful.

For Sanjay, let's hope that he finds something that he can enjoy doing and may his parents be strong enough to go through these tough times. They, unknowingly, contributed in the making of the Sanjay of today.

The parents have become very aloof, sad, and feel guilty. Whenever they get an opportunity, they try to sensitize other parents to the fact that they should let their children follow their own little dreams rather than brushing them aside and working to fulfil their parents' dreams.

Reflections

As parents, we aspire to give the best to our children. However, in this process, some of us, unknowingly, choose dreams and goals based on our knowledge or based on what others are doing. We then start forcing our unfulfilled desires and dreams on our children. So we force them to accept what we think they should become, or what stream should they choose, or what careers they should follow. In this parenting role, we forget that each child is an individual who is unique, with his or her own preferences, intelligence, and inherent nature. Our duty as parents is to provide an environment where our children can freely explore, experiment, analyse, and learn and in this process, discover their passion and make a profession out of it.

Gone are the days when the only career choices were limited to Engineer, Doctor, Civil Servant, Armed Forces officer, and Banker. Today's children have numerous choices. The time has come for all parents to remove their biases and let some sunlight in. We have to develop our thinking and let our children investigate the unexplored fields. As parents, we need to provide all the ingredients for the holistic development of our children, that is, design the environment. But we should never push our children. Instead, we should give them directions and let them figure out and choose their own path.

I find Steven Rudolph's multiple nature theory very relevant here. This theory will prove to be a great tool in the hands of today's parents to help their children discover the right careers for themselves. His book *Solving the Ice Cream Dilemma* is about helping your child choose the right career. I feel this is a logical and scientific approach. I recommend every parent to read this book.

Parents, we need to, unconditionally, accept our children as they are, have realistic expectations from them, and have faith and belief in them. It is only then that they will blossom. In the two stories mentioned above, the intentions of both the sets of parents were good, but what was the result? Did the parents ever want this kind of an outcome?

All parents want their children to be happy. We have to understand that life is not about being competitive all the time. It is about living your dreams and being happy. So, dear parents, be there with your children, by their side, and support them to explore and discover their own paths. But please never ever force your own dreams on your children. It becomes very difficult for them to handle this.

Howard Gardner identified eight intelligences or abilities that exist in differing degrees in all people. They are Bodily, Interpersonal, Logical, Linguistic, Visual, Musical, Intrapersonal, and Naturalistic. The relative strengths a person has among these intelligences provide a helpful guide to determine whether an individual is suitable for a particular line of work or career. For example, a fitness instructor would need strong Bodily intelligence.

The Multiple Nature (MN) theory by Steven Rudolph describes what people do, or are capable of doing, with the Multiple Intelligences (MIs) they possess. There are nine MNs that Steven has talked about. These are Protective, Educative, Administrative, Creative, Healing, Entertaining, Providing, Entrepreneurial, and Adventurous. Through his book he has attempted to help readers to identify their child's MNs and use this knowledge to guide the child along a path which will make the best use of his or her skills. Thus children can have personal fulfilment and happiness in their careers.

I feel each one of us wants our children to be happy and successful in life. So let us separate our dreams from theirs. We need to support and encourage our children to choose their own direction and purpose in life.

2
Why Did You Make Me a Cripple?

Mayank had scored 96 per cent in his boards. It was a dream come true for him and his parents. Now began a new chapter in Mayank's life. His dream of studying in Delhi University was about to be fulfilled.

Mayank got admission in the undergraduate programme of the college he wanted. Soon, all the admission related formalities were completed. The time had come for him to leave Chandigarh, his home town.

In the middle of all the excitement, there was a fear of having to stay alone and manage things by himself. Mayank had a lot of anxiety over getting separated from his parents, the new environment in the college, and all the other changes associated with his movement. It was the same for his parents. But there was no other way for Mayank except to move on and get geared up for a new life altogether.

Mayank and his parents had spent almost a week in Delhi before all the arrangements could be done. They had been exploring all the available options of boarding and lodging facilities, but were getting nowhere because Mayank did not approve of the places shown to him. Ultimately, a house was finalized. He had to live with a group of five other boys of the same college, who were also from Chandigarh.

Mayank's parents had carried some of the items required for his stay from Chandigarh and the others were purchased from Delhi. While the other parents left for Chandigarh, Mayank's parents stayed in a hotel and thought that they would go back after two days, when Mayank settled down with his new apartment mates.

On the first day Mayank found everything very challenging. There were three rooms in the house. They had to share the rooms because there were six of them. All the boys decided to pool in money to bring the groceries. Duties were assigned and rooms allotted. Everything seemed settled.

Mayank's mother came in the evening and kept all his clothes in the cupboard, along with some eatables. She arranged everything for him and told him where the various things were kept. In fact, she made a list and gave it to him so that he would not have problems finding his things.

All the other boys also appeared to have settled down. Since their accommodation was near the college, commuting was convenient. Near their apartment was a local shopping complex which catered to almost all the needs of the students. Mayank's parents boarded the train to return to Chandigarh, with a heavy heart. Their parting thoughts were that Mayank would definitely take a longer time than his other friends, but would finally get adjusted to his new college life and his routine.

It was almost the second week of the term and Mayank had got up late, again. He had been late many times earlier also. Once again he was late for his class. He rushed through, could not find fresh clothes and so wore the same ones that he had worn the day before. None of his clothes were washed, there was a pile of them, all dumped into one big heap. He could not find his bag, his phone was not charged, and there was nothing that he could eat for breakfast. He rushed and barely reached his college in time for the classes.

This situation was getting from bad to worse with each passing day. Mayank was highly disorganized, had no routine, could not complete his class assignments, and had no idea about managing his life. Other than studying, he felt everything else was a waste of time.

The whole house was littered with unwashed utensils, used clothes. The bathroom was dirty and smelly. It seemed the other five apartment mates could not also manage the house or themselves.

One day, in the evening, after dinner, Mayank raised this issue with his apartment mates and asked their views on a solution to all this mess. He wanted to know if the problem was with him only or if they were also facing the same issues. Each one then came out and shared his situation. Everyone was struggling with one problem or the other. And none of them knew what to do.

The major challenge faced by all of them was managing their money. They spent so much in the first week that lasting the entire month was almost impossible within the budget their parents had given. They had to borrow money from friends. They had no idea how to manage the groceries, how much and what quantity to purchase. They could not manage the washing and ironing of their clothes. Time management was a major challenge with all of them. Improper meal routines affected everyone. Nobody knew how to have a balanced diet. Last, but not the least, was the problem of getting into a self-study mode. At home, in Chandigarh, there were parents to wake you up and most of the studies were supported by tuition teachers. Now they were all facing the problem of completing their projects and assignments on their own in the stipulated time, because their parents had spoon-fed them until now. The discussion on this topic went on till about midnight, when they all dispersed, since they had to attend college the next day.

The next day, Mayank was coming out of his first lecture in the morning when he bumped into Sameer, an old schoolmate, who was a senior and in the final year of college. They went to the canteen, where they spent an hour catching up. Finally, when they were parting, Mayank shared his problem with his senior and wanted to know how he was managing his life.

Sameer replied that the first term was a mess for him also. He could not manage anything. It started impacting both his health and studies. So he shifted to a relative's place. Finally, in his second year, he had to call his mother to Delhi. Now they were staying in a rented apartment, where his mother manages everything for him. She keeps visiting Chandigarh off and on, because his father has a job there and cannot move to Delhi.

Mayank kept pondering about it all. Then, on his way back home, he called up his mother. He asked her, "Mom, why did you and Dad give me everything on a platter? You spoon-fed me and never allowed me to struggle for anything. Do you know what you, my parents, have done to me? You have made me a cripple! In the name of love, concern, and studies, you made me believe that everything thing else, other than studies, is a waste of time. You should know that all things other than studies are the life-skills which every individual needs to be good at. These skills are critical for survival. Why did you do this to me?" Mayank's mother did not know what to answer. She kept on wondering, "Where did my husband and I go wrong?"

Reflections

This is a common concern which most of our children face when they leave the comfort zone of their home to go out for studies. We, in the name of love and concern, hardly allow our children to do anything on their own, starting from feeding them, to taking care of their studies, to packing their bags, to getting their clothes ready, and so on. In the morning, it is a common sight, to see Moms and Dads go to the extent of carrying the school bags on their shoulders while escorting their children to the school bus. Little do we realize that, just like after boarding the bus they are on their own, after a certain age they will have to manage their lives on their own.

Another fact is that we will not always be around to protect our children and make sure they are safe. We, as parents, often do not let our children experience what it is to be independent. We are always ready to spoon-feed them. Our justification is that they are simply children, let them enjoy. Or, "I have only one child and I want to do the best for my child," or, "It is a competitive world. Children need to channelize their energies only into studies. The rest of the things, we as parents, will manage, so that our child does well in school and does not waste his or her time." Caught in these thoughts of ours, we forget that the entire aim of parenting, the aim of education, and the aim during the growing up years, is to make the children independent. But unfortunately, through our safe parenting practices, we make our children dependent and crippled. Parents, let us explore the opportunities to make our children more abled rather than disabled

The personality of our children is the end product of two components, that is, nature and nurture. Nature means the genes which a child inherits from his or her parents; nurture is everything that forms their environment.

Parents and the family is the first environment of the child. Every child sees the world through the eyes of his or her parents. Therefore a parent-child relationship is the basic foundation on which children build their life.

It is inappropriate, but in the name of competitive environment and survival of the fittest, in our country the parents give a lot of importance to academics. We feel that if the child does well by scoring high marks in school, he or she will be able to earn good money, which, according to us, is the key to success and happiness. So, while extracurricular activities are appreciated by parents, the main focus is on academics.

In the name of promoting academics, we often end up trying to make the environment as comfortable as possible for our children. They get everything ready-made, which results in their becoming highly dependent rather than becoming independent. At about 18 years, most of the children have to come out of their cocoons, that is, their comfort zone, and fend for themselves in college. Some of our children feel as if they have been pushed, to walk on their own without crutches, on weak legs.

Though our education system is going through an evolution, the basic life-skills, which are survival skills, are not a part of our curriculum. Skills like self-awareness, financial literacy, time management, and independent decision making are those without which an individual cannot survive, even though he or she may have the best college degree and the best marks. Therefore it becomes the responsibility of all parents not to cripple their children, but to empower them to walk independently.

Some of the strategies for helping our children to be independent are:

1. Stop overprotecting the children. Let them experience life and learn their lessons. Otherwise, they will always be dependent and will always seek guidance. Decision making, then, will become a challenge for them. This will make them a "safe player" and a "people pleaser" and interfere and restrict their emotional intelligence.
2. Stop doubting your children. Have unconditional faith and belief in them. Whenever you are bothered or you have a doubt, have a heart-to heart-talk with your child. Look for solutions together.
3. Do not punish your children physically. Refrain from any kind of physical or emotional abuse because it might damage your children's cognitive development, hamper their self-esteem, and lower their confidence. As a result, your children might become total rebels or go on accepting everything like a doormat.
4. Have realistic expectations from your children. Otherwise they will feel frustrated and believe they are not good enough, which will push them into a state of depression. So value your children and have realistic, achievable expectations.
5. Never ever compare your children with others or among themselves. Nor allow well-meaning relatives and friends to do so. Instead, empathize with them, try to know how they feel and what they are going through. Children, who have always been compared with others, often develop feeling of worthlessness and low self-esteem.
6. Involve yourself meaningfully in your child's life. Don't become passive parents and allow everything to happen on its own. Critical feedback from parents

is important. To build the character of the children, it is the duty of parents to give them a fair evaluation so that they can accept their mistakes and learn to accept positive criticism in their stride.

7. Let children develop the skill of decision making and practice autonomy at home. Instead of deciding for them what clothes they should wear, what subject stream they should choose, what college they should go to, and what course they should take, involve them in the evaluation process and allow them to take decisions. Start from the early formative years, when children want to be independent. In the name of love and affection, we should not make our children completely dependent on us.

8. Never ever force your unfulfilled dreams and desires on your children. Instead, let them recognize and pursue their dreams and be responsible for them.

9. It is our responsibility to let our children experience risk. Children fall a few times before they learn to walk. We need to overcome our anxieties and support our children when they want to do something new. Risk taking is an essential quality of being a leader. If we remove this quality from our children, they will not be able to maximize their potential, because we never gave them a chance.

10. As parents, let us give freedom to our children to experience hardships and allow them to solve their own problems, instead of trying to fix everything for them. If we solve all the problems for them and not let them face the consequences of their actions, they will never learn to stand on their own feet.

11. Let our children hear "No" from us when required. We do not always have to bend to their wishes. Let them learn to argue in a logical manner and fight for what they really value and need.
12. Let us not reward good marks or high percentage with material gifts. Otherwise, the children will feel that they are doing a favour to their parents by studying. Later on, they might feel the same when they are working in a job, which will be very harmful. Instead, children need to feel intrinsically motivated and unconditionally loved so that they study and do a good job. They need to learn that they are doing it all for themselves and not for others.
13. As parents, we need to walk the talk. We need to set an example and live the life which we want our children to live.

As parents, we need to look at and value long term growth of our children instead of short term comfort. Parental love and affection is extremely important for children, but we need to make sure that it does not become a hindrance in their growth and development.

Parenting is like flying a kite. While you keep the control in your hands, you need to give space and freedom to the kite to fly and soar. You also need to protect it from the vagaries of nature.

We need to let our children develop life-skills from the very beginning so that when they move on independently in their life, they feel enriched, equipped, and empowered rather than crippled. The best training ground is home and the best trainers for instilling life-skills are parents.

I will conclude by sharing this wonderful story from Indian folklore.

The Caterpillar and the Butterfly

A man found a cocoon of a butterfly. One day, a small opening appeared in the cocoon. Fascinated, he sat and watched the caterpillar for several hours as it struggled to force its body through the little hole. Then it seemed to stop making any progress. It appeared as if it had gone as far as it could and could go no farther. After waiting for some time, the man decided to help the caterpillar. He took a pair of scissors and snipped the remaining bit of the cocoon. The caterpillar then emerged easily. But alas, it did not unfurl its wings and fly away gracefully. The butterfly had a swollen body and shrivelled wings.

The man continued to watch the butterfly, hoping that the wings would enlarge and expand to be able to support the body, which would contract in time. Neither happened. In fact, the butterfly spent the rest of its life crawling around with a swollen body and deformed wings. It was never able to fly.

What the man, in his kindness and haste, did not understand was that the restricting cocoon and the struggle required for the caterpillar to get through the small opening of the cocoon are nature's way of forcing fluid from the body of the caterpillar into its wings, so that it would be ready for flight once it achieved its freedom from the cocoon.

Upon reflection, we can say that sometimes struggles are exactly what our children need. Life without obstacles might cripple our children. They would not be as strong as they could have been, so let's allow our children to go through the challenges and struggles required, so that they can get strengthened and equipped for their life's journey.

3

PTM — Not Again!

Raman was anxious and restless. All through the night, he kept on tossing and turning in his bed. However hard he tried, he could not sleep. Sometimes he would check his Facebook account or the WhatsApp messages. To pass time, he finally, plugged on his new headphones, which his aunt had brought as a gift for him from US. Listening to music helped him relax. Finally, he started feeling sleepy. He removed the headphones, switched off the light, and went to sleep. The time was 4.30 a.m. There was still time, there were still four hours left for the most dreadful moment of his life, that is, attending of the Parents Teachers Meeting (PTM) with his Mom and Dad.

He woke up when his Mom switched on the light of his room and said, "Raman, it is already 7 a.m. Come on, get up! We have to get ready, so that at least on this PTM we are on time."

PTM! This word startled Raman and he got up at once. There was sweat on his forehead. He had been in the middle of a dream — a very scary dream! He dreamt he was on the top of a very steep mountain. While he was trying to look around, something happened and he fell. His whole body went falling — down, deep down. His stomach was churning, he had a sinking feeling. Raman often saw this dream during his sleep. It frightened him, sometimes to such an extent that he would dread going to sleep and forcibly kept himself awake.

Time was running fast. Raman and his parents were soon ready. At 8.30 a.m. they were at the school. The corridors of the school were overflowing with children and their parents. In the classrooms, the teachers were sitting with parents, discussing their children. It was the great, grand PTM, the wondrous Parent Teacher Meet!

Raman and his parents had to wait barely for five minutes before it was their turn — the most dreaded moment of Raman's life. The meeting began, the class teacher looked at Raman as if he had committed a crime and said sarcastically, "So Raman, should I discuss all the complaints that I have?" She started, "Mr and Mrs Singh, I don't know from where to begin. I have a long list of complaints against your son. He is very talkative. He cannot sit in his place for long. After every period he needs either to go to the washroom or to drink water. You must meet the English teacher. She wants to meet both of you because he is always laughing in her class. In the Math's class he was found drawing some pictures and in the Hindi class, which is generally before break time, your son has often been found eating his tiffin. Mr and Mrs Singh, please tell me, what should we do?"

When Mr and Mrs Singh spoke, Raman stood speechless, with his head down. His parents took the teacher's side and started scolding him, "Why do we always get to hear so many complaints against you? We send you to study. Why do you talk so much in the class? What is so funny in the English class? Why do you laugh all the time? Why can't you go to the washroom in the interval? You carry a bottle of water from home, so why do you have to go out to drink water? Did we ever tell you to have your tiffin in the class?" The scolding went on and on and on. Whenever Raman tried to justify himself or give his point of view, he was asked to be quiet either by the teacher or by the parents. Raman felt as if he was beneath a bulldozer.

PTM – Not Again!

Every time there was a PTM, Raman always dreaded it. He was sleepless the night before the PTM and had more sleepless nights after it, because he would get a dressing-down from his parents in front of the teacher and also when they got back home. The parents always questioned Raman why they only got to hear complaints against him, which embarrassed them, and they felt miserable in front of the teacher. Long lectures were administered to him after every PTM and all this resulted in Raman feeling sad and ashamed that he could not make his parents feel proud about him. He felt he was no good and could never ever make his parents happy. Unknowingly, his teachers and parents were hurting his self-esteem time and again. Unfortunately, the message which Raman got from these two sets of significant, impactful adults was that he was good for nothing. He felt sad and depressed. Year after year, in spite of working hard, his self-esteem declined further.

Though Raman would always be among the top ten students of the class, however hard he tried he could not come first. His parents were never satisfied with his marks and his position in the class. On top of that, because of the complaints at the PTM, they were never happy with Raman. As a result, he started believing that he was useless, in spite of the fact that academically he was always a good performer. But because his parents never appreciated his efforts and always kept telling him he could have done better, he lost confidence in himself.

Over a period of time, his marks started declining. He started withdrawing from his friends as well. He began looking for opportunities to miss school on some pretext or the other. He started bunking school and hanging around with friends who were into bad habits like smoking. When Raman was in Class 10, in the PTM his parents came to know of his poor academic performance and his change in behaviour.

His mother discussed the problem with her best friend, who said she knew a counsellor and advised her to seek her help. A meeting was fixed. When the counsellor explored the history of Raman's academic downfall, what came out was a big shock and an eye-opener for his parents. The counsellor found that, through the PTMs, which are meant to strengthen the self-esteem of the child by supporting, guiding, brainstorming, and problem-solving, both the parents and teachers unfortunately ended up hurting and lowering the self-esteem of the child. As a result, the child lost his confidence. He always felt guilty, as if he had committed a crime, because he could not fulfil the expectations of his parents and always embarrassed them at the PTMs. So he started suffering from constant anxiety, which would rise manifold around PTMs. Even his dreams, in which he saw himself falling, were an extension of this low self-esteem. Nobody, neither the parents nor the teachers ever appreciated what Raman was good at. They only highlighted his weaknesses without giving any attention to his strengths.

The counsellor also met the class teacher and counselled her. She counselled the parents separately and also together with the teacher. The child went for regular counselling sessions. A plan was devised for Raman, with the goal of building and strengthening his self-esteem, which had to be supported both by the parents and the teacher. The counsellor mediated and made the parents and the teacher work in collaboration with each other, to bring out the best in the child.

The counselling process started six months ago. The child is showing positive changes and has started looking forward to going to school. The parents have started spending considerable time with their son. The teachers are focusing on appreciating all that Raman is good at. Thankfully, his preparations for his Class 10 final examinations are going well. We can only wish him luck.

Reflections

It is unfortunate, but I have often seen that somehow the child becomes the soft victim in the name of PTMs. It is so sad to see children standing, with their heads down, and getting sandwiched between the comments of the parents and the teachers. This state of the children has always created discomfort. It has made me think, "What is the purpose of this great and grand Parent Teacher Meet?" A lot of parents have also shared this with me during my career as a counsellor.

In some educational institutions, the situation is made more complicated. The parents are made to sit in the class to which their child belongs and the PTM is held there. Thus, by association, the child is reminded every day, subsequently, of what happened during the PTM.

All the parents of other children also get to see and hear what is being discussed. The result is that the child feels publicly humiliated and the parents feel very embarrassed. This was never the objective of PTMs.

The best gift that we can give to our children is a healthy self-esteem. So, as parents and as educators, we need to make sure that the school and home are places where our children feel secure enough to explore, develop their potential, and grow as individuals. The purpose of a Parent Teacher Meet, which is what parents and teachers should aim to achieve, is to share the goal of helping the child learn life-skills in a positive environment. They should feel confident and become successful, not only in the academic domain, but successful in all the other developmental domains.

Research conducted recently has validated that when parents and teachers work together collaboratively, there is benefit to all involved, that is, students to earn higher grades, perform better in the tests, enthusiastically attend school, behave responsibly, and exhibit a positive attitude towards self, parents and school.

But, unfortunately, collaboration between parents and teachers is not always beneficial for the child—the way it happened with Raman. Be ready to collaborate, not attack or defend. In the case of Raman, teachers and parents collaborated, but unknowingly started attacking the self-esteem of the child. This happened with the child repeatedly. In some other cases, parents sometimes become angry or defensive and the PTMs end in a blame game.

Often, in a PTM teachers report only the bad behaviour of the child, that is, their complaints with the child, with the intent to help the child do better. Their purpose is not to put the blame on the parents or the child. But it does not get communicated like that. They are viewed as authoritative, sarcastic, and at times aggressive.

Ideally, nothing of this sort should happen. But if it does, dear parents, assume that the teacher is concerned about the learning and development of your child genuinely. Therefore, respond calmly and tactfully. Parents, during your interaction with the teacher, be empathetic. Through your words and deeds, show that you are genuinely concerned. Use the meeting to look for solutions and help the child to succeed.

Parents should remember that PTMs are not easy for teachers as well. The teachers are afraid and reluctant to give negative feedback in the form of complaints.

As aware and empowered parents, it is your duty to ask the teacher directly, "What does my child do well in the class?" If the teacher is unable to give any positive feedback or appreciate the child, you will have to help him or her discover the strengths of your child. For that you should have a list of the strengths of your child. It will be very helpful if you thanked and complimented the teachers for their efforts and let them know that you appreciate their intent of trying to help the child, even when it does not seem to be working.

As parents, it is our responsibility to love our children unconditionally and be by their side through thick and thin. Raman's parents could have assertively tried to safeguard the self-esteem of their child by appreciating what he was good at and communicating it to the teachers. This would have motivated the teachers to talk about the strengths of the child, which would have strengthened Raman's self-esteem.

The actual fact is that, as parents, we do not understand our role in the PTM. At times, PTMs become a one-sided affair, where only one significant adult is participating, that is, only the teacher, with a box full of complaints, is talking. It is important to hear out the teacher's concerns, but at the same time, it is important to participate in this collaborative forum.

To err is human. Sometimes teachers can also make mistakes and mix up reports. If you are an involved parent, you will come to know immediately. In that case, calmly highlight the fact, rather than getting into a blame game.

Do not get sucked into the situation of endless criticisms and unknowingly start lowering the self-esteem of your child. Do not be impulsive in PTMs. Be patient, hear out the teacher, and see if the report given looks like your child's report. If not, discuss your concerns with the teacher.

In Raman's case, most of the complaints were very general, unlike the way they were presented. If Raman's parents had faith and belief in him, they would not have been judgmental. Raman was actually a very intelligent, happy child, who was a kinaesthetic learner. His need was movement after short intervals. As significant adults, that is, as parents and teachers, if we give attention to the positive behaviour of our children and appreciate them for their good deeds, then the good deeds of our children are likely to increase.

Dear parents, become active participants and not simply listeners. Contribute in a productive way in the PTMs. Also, never ever start rebuking the child in front of the teachers and other parents or children. Correct the child in private, when you have reached home. Always give him or her a chance to explain his or her side of the story.

Mentioned below are some of the questions that can be put across to the teachers to know more about your child and his or her overall performance at school. But before that, be ready with a list of what your child is good at. Prepare yourself to talk about your child's actions outside school and his or her behaviour in the environment other than school.

1. Is my child able to understand the expectations of the teacher? Is the homework being done regularly?
2. How does my child respond socially? Is my child getting along with others? How are his or her interpersonal skills? Is there anything I need to know to be able to help my child?
3. How is my child's logic and reasoning in the situations he or she encounters?
4. What, according to you, are the strengths of my child? Please share an example.
5. What are the areas that we need to work upon? What are the weaknesses, or rather concerns, that we need to support?

6. How is his or her E.Q. (emotional quotient, that is, handling people and situations)?
7. Is my child curious? That is, does he or she ask questions?
8. Do you think my child is happy being at school?
9. Are there any behaviour concerns about my child that I need to know?
10. Do you think that my child is working to maximize his or her potential?
11. How does my child respond to assessments?
12. How can we support his or her learning and development at home?
13. Can we develop a plan to help my child and support his or her progress?

Parents and teachers, let us change the whole approach towards PTM by collaborating constructively to rediscover our children.

4

Don't Send Me to a Coaching School

Since the time Kshitij had got promoted to Class 9, the home environment had become extremely disturbed. The only topic of discussion at any time was, what will Kshitij take after Class 10. Engineering was something which came naturally to his parents' mind, because both of them were engineers. Since Kshitij was a bright child and got good marks in Science, they would often call him an engineer from the time he was four years old. Kshitij would also tell relatives and friends, proudly, that when he grew up, he would become an engineer like his parents. The whole house was gearing up for a new engineer in the family.

Taking the Science stream by Kshitij was automatic. While he was giving his Class 10 examinations, the parents were uncomfortable that since both of them were working, Kshitij was alone at home after school. They wondered who would take care of preparations for his engineering entrance examinations. Even if he joined a coaching institute, the commuting would take a lot of time.

They discussed the matter with his friend Arman's parents also. Kshitij and Arman were good friends—they had been together in the same class from nursery. After a lot of brainstorming, the two sets of parents finally reached a conclusion that sending them to a residential coaching institute would be best. The two children would be away from all distractions and they would get a controlled environment, where every child aimed for getting into the best of the engineering colleges.

The general agreement amongst the parents was that since life thrives on competition, it would be a great idea to introduce their children to that environment from Class 11 itself. So they somehow convinced their sons to go to a residential coaching institute in another town. The children also got excited, since they would get the best competitive environment which would help them to prepare for the engineering entrance exams after Class 12.

By the time the results of Class 10 were declared, most of the formalities for admission had been completed. Both the children were admitted to a very popular residential coaching institute. In the entrance exam to this coaching institute, both the children had scored above 95 per cent marks and earned scholarships.

Kshitij and Arman did well in Class 10 boards. They got a CGPA of 10. Clearing the entrance exam of the coaching institute and earning a scholarship gave them an extra boost to their motivation. There was excitement in both the households, with the last minute packing of the bags of the children.

Finally, both the friends started studying at the coaching institute. The first three months were great. The two did well in all the assessments conducted there, due to which they were put in the Alpha 1 batch, which was the batch with the best students and the best teachers. But by the fourth month, the two friends got shuffled because of the weekly ranking. While Arman continued to retain his position in Alpha 1, Kshitij could not manage and went to Alpha 3.

This was the time when Kshitij's parents met him for the first time after he had joined the coaching institute. They saw that he was looking weaker. They got worried and gave him the option of coming back home and going back to his old school. But this was not so easy for Kshitij. He wanted to live up to his own expectations and told his parents that he would put in more hard work and get back to Alpha 1. Unfortunately, this did not happen and by September end he had further gone down to Charlie 3 class.

One day Kshitij's parents got a call from the head of the coaching institute that their son was unwell and they must come immediately and take him back for treatment. His Mom and Dad asked him if he would like to go back home and Kshitij said an instant yes.

Once back home, Kshitij was taken to the family doctor, who found that his haemoglobin had gown down to 8 and he had a fluctuating blood pressure. After he recovered, he got admitted to Class 11 in the Science stream in his previous school. He passed his final exams with a lot of effort and was promoted to Class 12.

The parents felt very guilty about the whole affair because Kshitij, after coming back from the residential coaching institute, was a changed person. He did not have friends, was not interested in playing cricket, did not log on to Facebook, remained very anxious, got irritable, and felt he was no good. They were very worried, so they decided to go for professional counselling.

The counsellor's findings and analysis were that Kshitij felt frustrated and had a very low opinion of himself. Though he had an inclination towards Science and was interested in Engineering, the unrealistic expectations of his parents and the extremely structured and rigidly competitive environment of the residential coaching institute was something that he could not cope with. The unrealistic expectations and his failure to meet them brought his self-esteem down, due to which he lost his self-confidence.

The parents were counselled separately. They readily agreed to unconditionally support Kshitij. His mother left her job to be with her son. Kshitij and his parents decided not to take any kind of coaching for engineering entrance exams. He only studied for Class 12 boards.

Kshitij cleared his Class 12 with 75 per cent marks and got admitted in a private engineering college near his house. He has started going to the stadium for cricket practice and has now started socializing as well.

The parents are thankful to have their son back. They shared with the counsellor that all they wanted for their son was to see him happy.

Reflections

Recently, there has been a tremendous increase in the number of residential coaching institutes all across India. This increase is because more and more parents want to send their children to such institutes. The most recent and surprising additions are the ones taking children from Class 6 onwards, to prepare them for the competitive exams in the most unnatural way. And year after year, these institutes are churning out children who are making it to the best of engineering and medical colleges, thereby ensuring and attracting more and more students from all across India.

But not all the children from these institutes are lucky to complete their journey and reach their destination. Parents, it's time for us to reflect and not get caught in the rat race. Let us not succumb to the peer pressure to send our children to these institutes, unless and until they are equipped to handle this kind of pressure. There are a lot of children who have to quit in the middle and have to return home—emotionally, physically, and mentally exhausted, like in the case of Kshitij.

In the early 1940s, George H. Reavis, then Assistant Superintendent of Cincinnati Public Schools, Ohio, wrote a call to action. He called it "The Animal School". This was originally written for the Public School Bulletin. The Animal School has become a timeless and, as the reader will discover, timely allegory about the dangers inherent in blind evaluation policies.

The Animal School

Once upon a time, the animals had a school. The curriculum consisted of running, climbing, flying, and swimming. All of the animals took all the subjects.

The duck was good in swimming, better than the instructor and made passing grade in flying, but was practically hopeless in running. She was made to stay after school and drop her swimming class in order to practice running. She kept this up and finally became only average in swimming due to lack of practice. But, average was acceptable, so nobody worried about it except the duck.

The eagle was considered a problem pupil and was disciplined severely. She beat all the others to the top of the tree in the climbing class, but used her own way of getting there— she didn't use her feet.

The rabbit started out at the top of the class in running, but had a nervous breakdown and dropped out of school because of so much make-up work in swimming.

The squirrel led the climbing class, but the flying teacher made him start his flying lessons from the ground instead of the top of the tree. He developed leg cramps from over exertion at the take-off. He started getting Cs in climbing and Ds in running.

The practical prairie dogs apprenticed their offspring to a badger when the school authorities refused to add digging to the curriculum.

At the end of the year, an eel that could swim well, but run, climb, and fly only a little, topped the class and was made the valedictorian.

The moral of this fable is that each child is unique. Numerous assessments, achievement test scores, and IQ screenings confirm this fact. Therefore we, the responsible adults, need to recognize each child as an individual learner and provide an environment to discover his or her strengths. We need to allow our children to explore possibilities of new careers, because it is our responsibility not to produce just average technocrats, bureaucrats, doctors, teachers, and so on. When our children are supported and guided, the road they take might be less travelled, they might face more hurdles, but, in the end, they would be happy in the course they would be studying and the careers they would choose.

We, the parents, want the best for our children. We don't like to take a risk about their welfare. Through our development and experience, we have got conditioned to play safe. We often get easily affected by the pressures of this competitive world. However, if we continue in this manner, our children might get stuck in professions they didn't want to be in. Let us challenge our "safety first" thinking patterns, remove our blinkers, let more light in, and rediscover our children and their true potential in this new light.

Children learn best when we, the significant adults, that is, teachers and parents, develop and challenge their strengths and identify and support them in their weaknesses.

5

Why Don't You Listen to Me, Mom?

Mona was a very happy-go-lucky 18 year old girl, who had just joined college and was enjoying every moment of her life. She stayed in a joint family with her uncle, aunt, cousins, grandparents, and her own parents. Mona had an elder sister, Shivani, who was seven years older to her. She had got married a year ago and was living in the same town with her husband. Mona loved her family and she was very fond of her sister and brother-in-law. Whenever Mona's mother and father had to go out of town, Mona's mother would send her to stay at her sister's place.

But this time when Mona's Mom asked her to pack her bags to go and stay at her sister's house when they would be leaving for the US, Mona became very irritable and told her Mom that she would not go to her sister's place ever and, instead, she would stay at home.

Though theirs was a joint family, each family stayed on a separate floor and had separate entrances. Therefore, leaving Mona alone at home was the last option her parents would have been comfortable with. When the argument between the mother and daughter could not get settled, Mona, just for the satisfaction of her mother, suggested, "If you don't want me to stay alone, fine. I will go and stay with my best friend, Gini." Mona's mother, by this time, had exhausted all her patience and started with her usual lecture about "I fail to understand you" and "How can you enjoy so much with your friends, but when it comes to relatives, you simply don't seem to be interested." Mona was adamant about her decision and her parents had to board their flight with a heavy heart, leaving Mona to stay alone in the house.

Once Mona's parents returned, life was back on track—there were family dinners and get-togethers at the relatives or sometimes at their place, but life for Mona had changed. She was always in an irritated mood, she talked rudely with her relatives, disrespected them, and did not participate in any of the family functions. Mona's parents thought that she was turning into a rebel and was giving them a tough time. Mona's mother was very upset with this new unsociable behaviour of Mona, but her father was a level-headed person and felt Mona was just going through her own challenges and needed space. He felt she would soon be back to her usual self.

But when this changed behaviour continued for more than three months, even her Dad got worried. The parents had a detailed discussion among themselves, but whatever actions they tried to take, it bounced back at them.

One day, when Mona's Mom asked her to go to her Aunt's place where all her cousins were coming to spend some time together, she refused bluntly. And then, in a trembling voice, shared with her Mom the awful fact. When they had gone for the wedding of her cousin sister, Krishna, and while all the cousins were sleeping together, Kitty Aunty's son, Rahul, had tried touching her at the wrong places. When she tried to raise an alarm, he quickly went back to sleep. Kitty was Mona's mother's real sister and Rahul was her first cousin.

Mona's mother, instead of supporting her and empathizing with her, brushed off such a major, sensitive incident by saying, "Come on, Mona, don't be so dramatic. It must have been by accident that Rahul's hand touched you. He can never do such a thing intentionally." And she scolded Mona and warned her not to share this made-up incident with anyone else. She also accused Mona of attempting to spoil her relations with her relatives.

Mona was shocked beyond her wildest imagination. Her own mother did not support her! She felt suffocated. She did not have dinner and sobbed all night. Next morning, when she went to college, it was such a relief. She did not feel like going back home that day. She wanted to run away, but didn't know where to go.

Mona, by now, had started hating her mother. Their relationship deteriorated and they came to a point where they hardly talked to each other. Mona felt more happy and safe outside her home than within her circle of relatives. She continuously fought with her mother for more night-outs with her friends.

One day she shared the whole incident with her best friend and asked for her advice, because she had almost decided that she could not stay with her mother any longer, even for one more day. Luckily, this friend knew of a counsellor who had counselled her on many occasions and was a good friend of her mother.

An appointment was fixed and Mona went for counselling. The shocking truth was revealed in the three sessions that she had with the counsellor. Mona had been a victim of child sex abuse by her relatives.

Between her constant sobs, Mona went on pouring her heart out to this counsellor and her story can give goose pimples to anyone. Since her childhood days, she was being touched at the wrong places by her uncle, her Dad's elder brother. When she protested and resisted, he scared her by saying, "If you go to your Mom and Dad, they will not believe you. Instead, you will be called a bad girl for talking about dirty things not meant for children." Luckily, Mona was saved from actually being sexually abused because she was able to avoid her uncle and did not let him come close to her.

The next incident was her cousin trying to touch her at the wrong places and when she tried to share this with her Mom, she was shocked at how her own mother had reacted.

The third, and the most horrifying experience, which she had recently encountered, was with her brother-in-law, who was always flirting with her and looking for opportunities to call her to his house on some pretext or the other. All this was routed through his mother-in-law, that is, Mona's mother. Mona's sister was having trouble in her relationship with her husband since she had come to know of her husband's flirtatious actions, not only with Mona but a lot of other women also. Her sister was seriously thinking a divorce. Mona was in a fix. She did not know what to do. She felt that if she revealed the truth, it would ruin the relationship of her sister and her husband for life. The happiness of their family would vanish forever. And knowing her mother, she felt that all the blame would be put on her.

The counselling proved very useful for Mona. The counsellor called up the parents. They were counselled separately and then they were all counselled together.

The positive result from this counselling process was the acceptance of the facts by the parents. Mona's Dad was more open about his feelings. Her Mom felt so guilty that she almost went into a state of acute depression when she realised what her child had been actually going through. She confessed to the counsellor that she was so afraid that she did not know how to react. She was also scared that if these things came out in the open, they would spoil the family relationships for ever. She was also scared about what the society would say. The family's reputation was at stake. So she wanted to hush up the whole affair by not validating the incident.

Let us pray that girls like Mona get heard and understood by their parents. The parents need to be actively involved to stop this sexual victimization of their children by their so-called trusted family members.

Reflections

Parents, you are your child's world, the most lovable and trusted persons for your child. One of the most important duty of yours is to listen to them, know what is happening in their life, believe in what they say, and unconditionally love and support them. This should be the oath taken by all adults the moment they become parents.

Unfortunately, in this story, Mona's parents, in spite of being around at home, could not involve themselves properly in this sacred task of parenting. And when she, after lot of thinking, gathered courage to share her woes with her Mom, she got no validation of what she had gone through. Instead, such a sensitive issue was casually brushed aside by her Mom and she was accused and blamed as a person who wanted to spoil the relationships between the family members.

This is the worst thing that can happen to any child. Validation of the feelings of our children is the most important of our responsibilities as parents, because if we do not validate the feelings of our children, who will? Mona felt shattered, confused, and guilty about something which she was not at fault in any way.

A very important duty of parents is to protect their children. Child sex abuse is one of the biggest threats that we have to deal with in today's times. The first ever National Study on Child Abuse in India was conducted in April 2007 and released by the Ministry for Women and Child Development

(MWCD). According to this study, 53 per cent children in India have been abused at least once in their lifetime, out of which 50 per cent abusers were well known to the children, either as a family member or a person in a position of trust. Girls and boys are at an equal risk when it comes to child sex abuse.

The way to deal with this menace is, first, to accept the ugly fact that there is a constant threat of child sex abuse always lurking around us. We need to open our eyes and accept reality. We, as parents, cannot always be around to protect our children. So let us empower and equip our children to handle this challenge.

Guidelines for keeping children safe and sensitizing them about "Good touch" and "Bad touch"

1. Be aware of your child's environment when you are not with them.
2. Teach your children the correct names of their private body parts, as early as when they are 18 months old, when you start teaching them the names of all other body parts.
3. Set rules about places they may go, people they may meet, and things they may do. However, while setting limits to what they can do, give them the logic or reasoning. Make sure do not scare them in this process.
4. Respect children's feelings. Stop tickling them, squeezing their cheeks, or hugging them if they don't like it. This will help children set their boundaries. When adults at home respect their children's boundaries, the children learn to say "Stop" or "No"

to touch that makes them feel uncomfortable. This is very important.
5. Affirm and satisfy the emotional needs of children to whatever level possible.
6. Teach them how to respect adults, but at the same time, not to obey them at all times. Support and encourage your children to disagree with an adult who is trying to bully them.
7. Disseminate information about sex and sexual abuse in a balanced way, which is age-appropriate.
8. Encourage them to share their feelings and validate their emotions, always. Help them to express how they feel.
9. Play "What if" games with the child. Give examples of situations that the child could be in and practise what the best response should be.
Examples:
What if you are in the park and someone lifts your dress?
What if you are there in the market with mother and you can't find mother?
What if you are at a birthday party and an uncle puts you in his lap and you feel uncomfortable?
10. Don't leave the child unsupervised for long periods as this can open the doors to abuse. Check on your child regularly.
11. Stay involved and do not delegate key care-giving responsibilities to a third person unless he or she is trustworthy.
12. Encourage open communication with your children to be able to understand and protect them. Discuss the body and its functions in a healthy, free-from-shame manner.
13. Above all, believe what your children tell you.

14. Books that can be used by parents to help teach their children about good touch and bad touch:
    Your Body Belongs to You by Cornelia Spelman
    Some Parts Are Not for Sharing by Julie K. Fredrico
    Do You Have a Secret? (Let's talk about it!) by Jennifer Moore-Mallinos
    I Can Play it Safe by Alison Feigh
    I Can Be Safe: A First Look at Safety by Pat Thomas (for ages 7 and above)
    Reena's Bollywood Dream: A Story about Sexual Abuse by Jewel Kats (for ages 7 and above)
    Uncle Willy's Tickles: A Child's Right to Say No by Marcie Aboff (a book for timid children)
15. The YouTube links that can be used by parents to sensitize their children are:
    http://www.youtube.com/watch?v=VkY0xqtw6W8
    http://www.youtube.com/watch?v=6aH8Rwax09A
    http://www.youtube.com/watch?v=4KWan3N-yhM

Parents, let us take a pledge together that, come what may, we will not let this menace spread. We will all make efforts to enhance our knowledge on this sensitive issue of child sex abuse and learn how to impart correct knowledge to our children so that they can get empowered and conscious to handle any situation in which they are caught by surprise.

6

Can You Ever Understand Me?

Raveena had just entered the house; she had come back from school. She had not even changed her dress when the arguments with her mother began. Her mother asked her why she had not made her bed in the morning and kept her clothes in the washtub — she went on and on. Raveena tried to justify herself. So the arguments started and went to a level where Raveena stomped her feet and walked out, saying, "Leave it Mom, you can never understand me!" Instead of letting the argument rest, Raveena's Mom walked into her room and reprimanded her, "Is this the way to talk to your Mom? I sacrificed my career to be with you and take care of you and you have grown so big that now you answer me back and argue with me!" Raveena retorted, "I did not ask you to leave your job, so don't tell me anything. I am no more a baby, I am a grown-up girl. I have a mind of my own. It is high time you grow up Mom and have the courage to listen to my point of view." Then she went into the washroom and locked the door behind her.

These fights had become a regular affair. And then the two would not talk to each other for days.

Raveena was the only child. Theirs was a nuclear family. Her mother was a stay-at-home Mom. Her Dad had a travelling job and was away for about 18 days in month.

Whenever Raveena's Dad returned from his tour, he would have to play the peacemaker between the mother and the daughter. He would often take side of his wife, which would make matters worse. One day Raveena went to the extent of telling her parents that she hated them and would run away from the house some day if they did not change their behaviour.

Once, when Raveena came back home from school and wanted to eat food in her room while watching her favourite programme *(How I Met Your Mother)*, her Mom did not let her do so. She forced her to eat lunch at the dining table. Raveena did not argue and quickly finished her meal. She was realizing that the best way to deal with her parents was to ignore them because they could never understand her. Her belief was getting stronger with each passing day.

When Raveena discussed with her parents the issues related to the Biology teacher, and how she was biased against her and always sarcastic, instead of making an effort to understand, her parents told her that all teachers need to be unconditionally respected. She must remain obedient to all of them, especially the Biology teacher. Otherwise it might impact her marks in Biology, because there are practicals in the subject, which are marked subjectively.

Raveena, as usual, tried to put her point of view across. Her teacher had been harassing her since long. But she was told, "You are just a child. You are not aware of the worldly ways, so listen to what your parents have to tell you. Behave properly with your teachers." "Oh, not again!" said Raveena. "Please, Mom and Dad, I am not at fault. It is my teacher who is at fault. I want you to come to school and address this problem of mine. Ms Priya, my Biology teacher, has no right to behave the way she does with me. Just because I don't agree with her and put my point of view across, she is always looking for opportunities to harass me. On some pretext or the other, she will make use of her authority and embarrass me by writing a note to you in the diary. Or she will take me to the Principal saying I was talking in class. Or she will punish me by making me stand outside the class because I did not bring the homework copy. There are other children who also do not bring their homework copies, but she does not punish them at all. Why always me? I am not going to take it any more. You have to come to my school and tell the Principal about it."

Raveena's father spoke firmly to her. He said, "This is not done. You are not a child any more. You should know how to deal with this. Just don't give your Biology teacher any opportunity to punish you. We will not go to the Principal. If we complain about this teacher, she will become more biased and spoil your practical and subject grades, which will not be good for you. When we were your age, even we had many complaints against our teachers. But we could not do anything, because they had our marks in their hands. It is a matter of only three months before the year is over. Somehow manage and then forget about all this." Raveena was furious. She felt isolated, helpless, and hurt. She cried for hours in her room.

That day she took a drastic step. She packed a small bag with her school dress, a night suit, and some toiletries. When her parents went out to the local shopping complex, she quietly slipped out of the house and went to her aunt's (her Mom's cousin) house. She did not take her mobile phone.

It was already dark and her aunt's house was 15 km away. While she was still on her way, her parents got back home, only to discover that Raveena was missing. They were very worried. They called a couple of her friends but did not get any information about her. They had almost decided to go to the police station to lodge a complaint, when the phone rang. The caller was Kavita, Raveena's aunt, who was in a state of shock. She informed the worried parents that Raveena was with her. She had reached her place a few minutes ago. When her parents wanted to talk to her, Raveena refused to talk. Her parents rushed to Kavita's house immediately to bring her back.

This incident came as a big shock to the whole family. Kavita called up a counsellor she knew. An appointment was fixed. The counsellor found that Raveena's parents always treated her as a small child, doubted her, and did not trust her. Whenever she shared anything with them, she was told that she had no idea or experience about anything in life. She was only expected to obey the instructions of parents and teachers, because only they had the complete understanding of the right and the wrong. Raveena felt frustrated when she was not given a hearing. She did not know what to do or where to go, because she was always misunderstood by her parents. She felt stifled, she wanted to run away, and thankfully she chose her aunt's place to go to.

The counsellor explained to Raveena that her parents' intentions were good, but probably they could not understand her feelings and could not validate them. That is why she felt that her parents never understood her. But they genuinely loved her and wanted the best for her. She also counselled the parents and tried to sensitize them as to how they needed to give space to such a grown-up child. They should control their own fears and have faith and belief in their daughter and stand by her.

Raveena's relationship with her parents has started becoming positive and the family is still working, along with the counsellor, to further strengthen it.

Reflections

This is not just Raveena's story. This is the situation in most households where children are growing up. Parents and children end up arguing all the time. They indulge in a power struggle. Where parents dominate their children, the children learn to play safe. As a result of these parenting practices, children either become rebellious and love challenging authority figures, or give in and become submissive, easily get bullied, and become "people pleasers". While, as parents, we do our best and want the best for our children, probably we do not know how to go about it.

The ultimate aim of parenting is to empower our children to be independent, thoughtful thinkers, who know how to live their life in a happy and peaceful manner. As parents, the most important tool which we can use to achieve this is through communication. It is unfortunate that this very channel got blocked in the case of Raveena. This is where the matter started slipping out of everybody's hands.

Communication is the key and the most effective tool of twenty first century parenting. Parents can make a real difference in the lives of their children by practicing effective communication. When the communication channels are open and the communication is two-way, it not only gives us an insight into the lives of our children, but also helps us to empower them.

It is extremely important for parents to be able to communicate effectively and openly with their children. The most important aspect of effective communication is to listen to what the children have to say or how they feel.

Children begin to form their self-concepts based on how their parents communicate with them. Therefore, when parents communicate effectively, by listening patiently, the message which goes to the children is that their parents respect them. So it is very essential that when our children are conveying their feelings and ideas and want to share their thoughts, they are encouraged to do so.

It is unfortunate that, as parents, we have been conditioned either to provide solutions, give suggestions, and advice, or become judgmental about whatever our children share with us. Instead, when parents engage in the simple task of effective communication by being empathetic listeners, children begin to feel they are heard and understood by their parents. This boosts their self-esteem. On the other hand, if the communication between the parents and their children is ineffective or negative, children start believing that they are not important, they feel ignored, or misunderstood. Children then start seeing their parents as unhelpful, unconcerned, and distrustful. With the break in communication, parents are unable to understand what the children are going through, as in the case of Raveena. During most of her conversations with her parents, unknowingly, the parents were conveying a message that how she feels and what she experiences was not important for them at all. She felt as though they hardly validated her presence in the house. She felt so repressed in such a family environment that she ran away from it. Fortunately, it was to her aunt's place. Otherwise this high risk behaviour could have resulted in a terrible situation.

When, as parents, we practice effective communication with our children, they are more likely to hear us out and be willing to do what is expected out of them. "Listening" in a way that you really understand what your children are saying and "talking" in a way that they really appreciate it, are the two of the best things you can do to help your children develop a high self-esteem and positive values.

Your children will definitely respond to your efforts to connect with them if you show that it really matters to you. So do it often, openly, and throughout the growing-up years. Children need to know that their parents are going to listen to them calmly and not react if a problem arises. They are more likely to close up and avoid seeking help and advice if they have an impression that you are going to react with anger or panic. In that case, they will go into a shell and will hesitate to share things with you.

Active listening is the key to keep the communication channels open. To be an active listener, as parents, you need to practise the following:

1. Listen to your children's spoken words as well as unspoken feelings and validate them.
2. Don't interrupt or let anyone else interrupt when your child is talking to you.
3. Don't engage yourself in any other thing when your child is speaking to you. Look at your child by making good eye contact and responding appropriately to show that you are listening.
4. Ask your child to explain if you don't understand his or her point of view. Express in statements that show that you have heard what your child said and that you understood his or her point of view.
5. Try to hear and respond to the feelings behind the statements made by your child. Don't try to guess what your child feels—if you don't understand ask him or her.
6. Use "I" messages instead of "You" messages that blame or belittle the child. For example, you can say, "Because I love you and because I care for you, I want you to be safe," rather than, "You are ignorant and silly, so I need to tell you how to be safe."

7. If either one of you, that is, you and your child, is not in the right frame of mind, ask if the discussion can wait. Then take it up as soon as possible. Make time from your schedule to talk about issues that are important to your child.
8. Try not to judge, but let your children know how you feel when they say something negative or become angry.
9. Don't feel you have to fix everything for your child. Children learn independence when they are involved in solving their own problems.

Effective listening is one of the most important ingredients of effective communication. In order to be effectively listening to your children, you need to give 100 per cent attention to them by removing all distractions. Let your children know that you are hearing by summarizing what they said after they have finished talking, keep your talks precise, and know when to back off.

Parents need to ask their children open ended questions, rather than interrogating them. Venting out time or emotional baggage decluttering can be scheduled once a week, when children are allowed to express how they felt in the previous week.

Don't reject the children's viewpoint outright. Encourage them to ask questions—give age-appropriate answers. Don't dominate them or force them to agree with your point of view. To have different points of view is absolutely acceptable.

If there are many concerns expressed at the same time, work on them one by one. Apply brainstorming and divergent thinking patterns to solve the problems. Use "I" messages to put across your point of view. Be respectful towards your children by being polite. Validate their feelings. Never ever lie to your children.

Encourage your children to talk by saying, "That's really interesting. Tell me, I want to hear you in detail. Is there anything else you want to talk about?" Say "I completely understand you" often during your conversation.

Some of the challenges of effective communication are:

1. When the parents bring in the past mistakes of the child.
2. When we are always trying to give solutions.
3. When we become critical, nag, and lecture the child.
4. When we don't let them talk and repeatedly go on interrupting.
5. When we try to control their behaviour by making them feel guilty, by being sarcastic, or by threatening them.

It's time for us to change our communication patterns and tune in to the frequency of our children, by not treating them like a baby. Instead, the interactions need to be age-appropriate.

7

Were You Ready for Me?

Jai felt depressed and very insecure. Once again his parents were shouting and arguing. The issue was, who would take leave to take Jai to the doctor, because both had an important meeting the next day. Jai quickly slipped out of the dining room and went in his room. He was very upset and started crying. His Mom and Dad heard him and came running into his room. They tried to console him. Both were desperate to know as to why was Jai crying so badly. Soon, the house gained its peace back and now Jai shared with his parents that he was feeling really bad—because of him, his Mom and Dad were fighting.

When Jai questioned them that if they had so many conflicts and did not have time for him, why did they give birth to him, they were speechless. They tried to justify, saying that all Moms and Dads have conflicts and fights. It's a normal part of life, there is nothing to feel so bad about it and talk to your parents like this. Finally, it was decided that Jai's Dad would take him to the doctor.

Even though there was peace in the outside environment, Jai's internal environment was very chaotic. He was feeling guilty. He felt bad that because of him there were regular fights between his Mom and Dad, due to which they could never be happy as a family.

That day Jai could not concentrate on his studies at all. When he tried sleeping, he could not sleep. He was anxious and frightened due to these conflicts between his parents. He wondered what would happen to him if his parents decide to split and get divorced. With whom would he live? He loved both of them. He kept wondering that if he decided to stay with his Mom, how his Dad would feel. At dinner time, he was very quiet and did not even notice what he was eating.

Since he was not well and had to go to the doctor, he could go to school only after two days. In the class, he was restless and could hardly concentrate on what was going on. He was engrossed in his own internal dialogues. Why do his parents fight? And what should he do about it?

The Maths teacher arrived and Jai did not even know what the homework was. He was punished and a note was sent to his parents, which made him more fearful. So Jai decided to forge his Dad's signature. He did not want to be the reason for his parents fight once again and be responsible for their conflict.

Jai was losing his focus on studies. He was often caught day-dreaming by his teachers and was blank when questioned.

His parents would only come back in the evening from work. They were always entangled in their own power struggles, where one would try to show the other down. Both could not spend much time with him.

In spite of the fact that he was in Class 9, he hardly had any friends. It was not that he did not have any friends ever, but as time passed by, he started losing them because he had become very sensitive. Even the slightest of disagreement led to the break-up of his relationship with his friends.

The final exams of Class 9 were just over three days ago, when Jai's Dad received a call from his class teacher that she wanted to meet both Jai's parents, together, to discuss her concerns regarding Jai. A similar call was received by Jai's

Mom as well. The next day Jai's parents were sitting with the school counsellor, trying to understand what went wrong due to which Jai had developed such a low self-esteem. He always underestimated himself, had conflicts with almost all his friends, remained quiet, looked depressed, and was always very anxious. His mental and emotional state had started becoming a hindrance to his overall growth and development. While in the past he was always in the top three, now he was nowhere even in the top ten.

The school counsellor had a detailed session and her findings were a very strong wake-up call for Jai's parents. According to her, Jai was in a state of depression and needed help at the earliest. She said that she has had four sessions with Jai and he had a lot to share with her.

Jai had been having problems with his sleep since the last two months. He did not feel like taking a bath, he did not feel like eating, earlier he used to have conflicts with his friends but then he started shying away from all of them, he had palpitations at times, he felt so insecure that he hated being alone, he wanted to hold on to an adult's hand, his bowel movements were irregular, he could not concentrate on his studies and though he learned the concepts, he become blank when he saw the examination paper. The list was endless.

The school counsellor asked the parents, "Do you know what has gone into his subconscious mind? He believes he is the root cause of all your conflicts and fights. He is always anxious that one day you will get separated. But since he loves you both, how would he handle your separation?"

The parents were deeply shocked by these revelations. Jai's Mom could not control her tears. Jai's Dad became numb and cold. Then the school counsellor's voice asking them a question startled them and brought them back to the reality of the situation they were in. They felt so ashamed of themselves, and so guilty, that they did not know where to look.

The counsellor advised them that from then onwards, they would have to work as a team to be able to bring back Jai's confidence and faith in their relationship and feel safe. But before that, she advised that Jai was in a state of acute depression and needed immediate medical intervention. He first needed to be able to switch off, relax, and sleep. She gave them the address of a Psychiatrist, who was a friend of hers, who could help them through family counselling sessions, as well as individual sessions.

The parents were extremely thankful to the school counsellor and followed her advice. They took Jai to the Psychiatrist referred by the school counsellor, who prescribed medicines which helped in restoring Jai's normal sleep pattern. His mother took a sabbatical for six months to look after him. She monitored his medicine schedules and psychotherapy sessions. Though the medication stopped after three months, the counselling sessions went for about six months.

With all this help, Jai bounced back to life and was able to recover fully. Their house did not witness the fights, shouts, and showdowns between his parents, as in the past. Both the parents worked on their relationship to resolve the conflicts which had so deeply impacted their child that he had become severely depressed. Thus, Jai's parents could assure Jai that they loved each other and they loved him and would always stay together.

Reflections

Jai was very lucky to get the intervention at the right time. But not everybody is so lucky. There are many children who become the victims of their parents' conflicts, which impacts their mental, emotional, and physical health and scars them for life.

Every child's expectation from his or her parents is that they love and respect each other and will remain together. Children feel extremely insecure and threatened when their parents argue nonstop and fight. The reason for fights may be related to both the sides of relatives, financial matters, kitchen matters, material desires, smoking, drinking, extramarital affairs, and so on. It is acceptable to have disagreements, differences of opinion, have different priorities, or have different beliefs because the parents may come from different belief systems, backgrounds, education, and environment. But when it comes to children, the parents need to work as a team.

One of the most important duty of parents is to provide the most conducive environment for the overall development of their children. They should use proper communication skills so that what each parent feels can be expressed in a healthy manner, without offending the other person.

In this story, Jai's parents could not communicate with each other with respect. This resulted in a continuous conflict between them. They would get into confrontation even for trivial reasons and then start shouting, screaming, blaming each other, being sarcastic, throwing things, using abusive language, and always trying to dominate each other.

Once we become parents, we become an integral part of the growing child's environment. Constant parental fights are called chronic parental conflicts. They have a major negative impact on the children, who are a witness to the entire process.

Some of the major impacts of parental conflict on children are:

1. Children feel insecure and unsafe because, for the child, parents provide the most important environment. If there are regular conflicts between

parents, the child starts imagining all sorts of negative things happening to him or her.
2. Children might suffer from diminishing self-esteem and exhibit behavioural problems like biting nails, bed-wetting, stuttering, stammering, and so on.
3. They become over anxious, emotionally drained, and extremely sensitive.
4. In some cases, children might suffer from inability to sleep, that is, insomnia, which finally results in depression.
5. For children, Mom and Dad are both important and they love them equally. It becomes very stressful for them to take sides when the parents fight.
6. Children start blaming themselves for the constant conflict amongst their parents, which might be due to their different parenting style, beliefs, or cultural backgrounds. Children become distressed because of the feelings of guilt and they don't know how to handle them.
7. Since parents are their child's world, children learn the maximum by observing and imitating them. When parents are engaged in unhealthy conflicts, they also may repeat the same behaviour. When any behaviour comes from parents, it readily gets absorbed by the children and it becomes a part of their personality.
8. Since both the parents are engrossed in their own conflicts, they are not able to constructively contribute to the task of parenting.
9. Relationships between children and their parents may get affected in the long run. Children will become reluctant to spend time with parents or would start avoiding them because they did not form a secure attachment with them during childhood.

10. They might get into substance abuse to numb their negative feelings.
11. Every child has an emotional bank. Regular conflicts between parents exhaust all the deposits of love, respect, belief and the child becomes emotionally bankrupt, making him or her very vulnerable to all kinds of emotional challenges.
12. Children find it difficult to adjust socially in any environment. They may remain maladjusted throughout their life. They may have weak interpersonal skills and weak problem solving abilities.
13. Some children might externalize their distress and become aggressive and impulsive in their behaviour.
14. The constant stress and anxiety which the children undergo may impact their brain development for life.

Conflict is a natural part of any relationship, but as parents we need to work together as a team to resolve conflicts in a constructive manner, because our children are watching us and learning life-skills from us. Let us explore some strategies to resolve these conflicts. This will help our children by giving them a secure and emotionally healthy environment:

1. Work together to resolve conflicts because you are your child's role model. When children see their parents working effectively through a problem, they learn problem solving skills; they learn to accept each other. They start accepting that disagreements between two adults are normal and that conflicts are healthy for brainstorming and finding the best solutions.
2. Keep your heated discussions away from children. Indulge in them behind closed doors or when your children are not around.

3. Resist being sucked into your never-ending conflicts. Instead, even while you are disagreeing with your partner, be affectionate to your children, listen to them, and talk to them about their life and interests. Reassure them through words and gestures that they are not the cause of their parents' conflicts.
4. Discourage your child to take sides, because this is not healthy for children in the long run. When a parent tries to team up with a child to put the other parent down, it is very harmful to the child's emotional balance. When the child realizes the truth, he or she will suffer from guilt throughout life. When one parent has withdrawn privileges in trying to correct the behaviour pattern of the child, if the other parent is not careful and does not validate the other parent, initially the child becomes confused. Later on, the child will smartly uses one parent against the other to get his or her unreasonable demands fulfilled. So working as a team is the only solution to avoid such complications, which will make the child into a highly manipulative adult. This will become a challenge during the personal and professional life of the child.
5. Refrain from leaning on your child's shoulder during times of such conflicts. Though he or she may appear to be handling it well, your child cannot be your emotional crutch. Children are not adults. Therefore their psychological development is yet not complete. It is not correct to burden them with your emotional baggage. Instead, let them see a mature adult in you, who knows how to handle his or her emotions, as well as those of others. If you have an urge to lean on a

shoulder, let it be of a professional counsellor, who is trained to handle your concerns.
6. Use effective communication skills to talk and resolve differences of opinions. Listen to each other without interrupting or being judgmental and use "I" statements in your conversations. Parents should restrict themselves to the present situation and not bring up the past while having a difference of opinion.
7. Talk and explain in brief to your children that Mom and Dad are having problems agreeing with each other, but they are making genuine efforts to sort out their differences. This might take time, but there is no reason to worry. Mom and Dad are fine and will always love you. Thus, children will not start having doubts.
8. Never ever give in to the temptation of criticizing the other parent in front of the children. This makes the children feel threatened about themselves, which might damage their self-esteem. Don't even talk ill about the other parent on phone or to someone else. Children might hear these conversations, which will cause great damage to your constructive parenting practices.

For parents, it is very important to take care of the child's environment. So they need to be extremely careful about the emotional state of the child. Practice empathy and communicate effectively to be able to give a healthy environment to your children because you, dear parents, are your child's world and the most impactful teacher.

Do You Trust Me on Money Matters?

Aman was nervous when he overheard his Dad talking on phone to someone from his school. He knew it was his class teacher, because she had told him that she would be calling his parents to discuss his recent PSP (PlayStation) episode. Aman was very scared. He knew that his parents would be called to the Principal's office the next day. This time, he knew, he could not escape punishment. Things were not in his hands now.

That day Aman's Dad looked very thoughtful, but he did not mention the phone call to him. The next day appeared to be a normal day, with the usual hustle and bustle of the morning. When Aman was about to step out of the house to catch his school bus, his Dad announced in a serious tone, "Aman, we will be there at school today to meet your class teacher and Principal to discuss the latest behaviour of yours." Aman could not stop himself from saying, "Sorry Dad, please give me one last chance. I will never embarrass you and Mom like this again. Please believe me, I have really not done anything. Dad, I want to tell you what actually happened." But Aman's Dad waved his hand to tell him to leave him and go to the school bus. It was clear that he was not willing to hear anything from Aman. He only said, "Don't worry, we will talk today once you are back from school."

The whole day Aman was very anxious and could not concentrate in class. He was dreading the time when he would be called to the Principal's office. There were many questions in his mind. What should he say? Should he tell the truth? Or should he hide the facts and hope for a lesser punishment? The whole day passed, but he was not called.

During this time, Aman's parents were sitting with the Principal. Ms Mary, Aman's class teacher, had also joined the discussions. She began the conversation and said, "Mr and Mrs Jain, we would like to inform you that Aman was caught playing with his PSP in the class by his Maths teacher. We have confiscated the PSP. Did he share anything with you?" Aman's parents were surprised. They had thought that this meeting would be regarding his academic performance, since he was in Class 10. The mention of PSP was a completely unexpected thing for them.

The Principal now addressed the parents and narrated the events. The whole story had been unravelled by the school counsellor. It seemed that ten days ago, on his way back home, Aman had found an expensive, brand new mobile phone, which he picked up and kept in his pocket. While he was thinking about what to do with the phone, an idea struck him. He decided that he would keep the phone with him. In case his parents asked, he would tell them that the phone belonged to his friend and he had carried it with him by mistake.

He explained the plan to his friend, who had always shared with him his dream of having a mobile phone for himself, but his parents were against the idea. Aman could relate to his friend, because he had always wanted a PSP but his parents did not agree. He had tried to convince his parents, but they said that the PSP would be a big distraction. Since he was in Class 10, he needed to concentrate on his studies. But Aman was obsessed. Having a PSP of his own had become Aman's dream and his strongest desire.

Then he had another idea. He gave the proposal to his friend, who wanted a mobile. He suggested to exchange the mobile with his friend's PSP. So Aman would have a PSP and his friend would have a mobile. At home, if asked, they would say it was their friend's and by mistake it had got carried home. Aman's friend agreed with the plan.

This went on for a few days. But, unfortunately, Aman got caught and the whole story came out in the open.

The school counsellor then reported a much bigger problem. She said that Aman felt frustrated and dejected, because for every little thing he wanted, he had to explain and convince his parents for hours. Even if he wanted to eat an ice-cream or buy something from the canteen, he had to beg for it, because his parents never gave him any pocket money.

Aman's parents told the Principal and the class teacher that they did not believe in the concept of pocket money. They said, "Without pocket money we are getting to hear so much, what would have happened with the pocket money? The moment children have power of money in their hands, they start to misuse it. So in the best interest of our child, we decided not to give him pocket money." They also believed that in this manner they could have some control on their child. They felt that since they were providing everything their son required, there was no need for pocket money, anyway.

On hearing this, the Principal explained to the parents, saying, "Your son is in Class 10 and needs to have financial literacy. You need to begin giving him pocket money so that he can learn how to manage his money. Show some trust and faith in him and his ability to handle money."

The parents were asked to meet the counsellor, who had a long session with them. Eventually, it was decided that a reasonable amount of pocket money should be given to Aman. The parents would guide him to save it and accumulate the amount needed to purchase his own PSP, or any other item that he wanted. It was also agreed that the parents would explain the virtue of honesty to Aman and the mobile found would be kept in the school, to trace the actual owner and return it to him.

That day, in the evening, Aman's parents sat with him and had a heart-to-heart talk with him, after which they gave him a decent allowance as pocket money and also told him how he could save it. Once he had enough money, he could buy his own PSP or anything else he wanted. Aman couldn't believe his ears! He was excited about his pocket money. Now he would not be deprived of fulfilling his little desires. He quickly started making his savings plan.

Aman's parents also talked to him at length about not keeping any lost item he found. He should give it to a person in authority to make efforts to return it to the rightful owner. Aman solemnly promised to always do so in the future.

Reflections

This is only one story. There are many others, where children have gone to the extent of stealing money to fulfil their day-to-day desires because the parents did not give any pocket money to them.

The matter is not only about fulfilling desires. Children learn to be responsible when they get pocket money. They learn the value and power of money. They develop financial literacy when they are allowed to handle money.

I remember of a friend of mine, who is 48 years old and is doing very well in her life professionally, but till now she is uncomfortable with money. She does not know how to handle her money, because as a child she was never given the exposure. Her parents did not trust her with money. Till today she believes that she cannot manage money. That is the kind of programming that she had as a child.

Financial literacy is an important skill in life. There is no subject better than financial literacy to empower our children on money matters. But this subject is not taught in schools. Therefore, it is all the more important for us, parents, to let our children access money, to be able to learn how to handle it in a productive manner.

Pocket money is a great way of helping children become financially literate from an early age. It also complements the maths education at school. The aim of parenting and schooling is to make our children move from dependence to independence. And financial independence is a major life-skill, the foundation of which has to start at an early age. Pocket money is the first step towards financial independence. How you spend, save and withdraw, lend, borrow, or donate money, all these transactions of the parents impact the child's learning about money.

As I have already mentioned in my previous book, children are like sponges and they absorb everything they come across. Since family is the first environment and you, parents, the first teachers, how you deal with money and how you talk about it sends messages to your children, which get absorbed in their subconscious minds and contribute to their attitude towards money throughout their life.

Children need to learn about the concept of money as early as possible. When we introduce this by giving them a fixed amount of allowance as pocket money, we are creating a platform for them to learn how to handle money. Though we have the best intentions, but at times we are confused and end up indulging in parenting practices which are more damaging than we can imagine. This is also because, unfortunately, we did not take a degree in parenting, nor do our children come with an instruction manual!

In the story we saw that Aman could have easily acquired financial literacy if he had been given an opportunity to experiment with money in the form of pocket money. But his parents felt that money will spoil him. After a particular age, we let our children take a bath on their own, dress up on their own, and eat on their own. Similarly, we have to have faith and trust in our children and let them deal with money on their own after a particular age.

Let us explore some basic issues about this much talked about concept of pocket money. With this awareness, you can maximize the benefits and help your children develop a healthy attitude towards money and make them financially literate.

1. It is important to teach them the difference between needs, wants, and desires. This will empower them to make appropriate spending decisions. The best way of teaching children is by being the correct role model and then talk about how you attend to your needs and how you restrict your wants and desires depending on the budget and the amount of money available.
2. The age at which you can start giving pocket money depends on you and your child's ability to make a sense of money. According to research, it is a great idea to introduce the concept of pocket money in your children's life by the time they are four years old, because by then they have developed a sense of their surroundings. They have become aware about the importance of money in their lives and that things are acquired by giving money.

3. Don't just give pocket money to your children randomly. Start building a conversation much before you actually give it. The conversation between you and your child needs to be open ended. You can ask your children what they will do with the pocket money. And why they want to do a particular thing. Also talk to them about the concept of saving for exigencies, giving examples from your life which they can relate to. Teach your children the concept of budgeting and help them to set goals for saving they may need for future.
4. Prepare your child, in advance, about the rules for pocket money, what all is it meant for, and what all it is not meant for. Don't shy away from addressing both. Let your children know about your expectations. Make the rules about how they spend their pocket money very clear. Also, let them know that if they do not behave responsibly with their pocket money, it would be withdrawn, till they become responsible. (Money, in that case, can be deposited in their name in their bank account).
5. Don't punish your children by withdrawing pocket money for long periods if they have done something wrong. Long withdrawal can cause a lot of resentment in children and can also be a reason for motivating them to steal money from their parents or from friends at school.
6. Be consistent. Have a fixed day to give pocket money. If it is weekly, then you could give it every Sunday; if monthly, then you could give it on the first of every month. Refrain from giving advance and resist from the urge to give them more if they have blown up all the money early.

7. However, allow your children to make financial mistakes. Do not try to influence, judge, or suggest. Just watch and observe, because this is how they will learn the pros and cons of making different types of financial decisions.
8. Parents, initially you need to be present with young children when they are spending money. For example, allow your child to spend a small amount on whatever he or she likes. Be observant and don't interrupt while the transaction is taking place. Later, discuss positives and negatives of the expense with your child.
9. Do not be tempted to give large amounts of pocket money to your children because of your guilt, to compensate for not being able to spend time with them. Do not give large amounts just because you can afford to do so. Children need to learn the value of small amounts of money also.
10. You need to keep a check on where your children are spending their pocket money. They may be tempted to spend it in improper ways. If you find anything inappropriate, confront your child and discuss. Do not shy from facing the problem upfront.
11. When you decide to give pocket money to your children, give them three piggy banks or jars. Label them as SOM, SOO, SFF, which stand for SOM=Spending on Me; SOO=Spending on Others; SFF=Saving for Future. Then guide them how to divide their pocket money in three parts and deposit in each jar, to be used accordingly. Once they have learnt how to save, get their account opened in a bank. For older children, you can let them handle their bank account themselves and their pocket money can be directly deposited there.

To sum up, we, as parents, must give an opportunity to our children to become financial literate and use pocket money as a tool to achieve it. Let us explore the role of pocket money in the overall development of our children:

1. When children get money to handle by way of pocket money, they not only feel good about it, but, over a period of time, become more responsible while using money.
2. When parents give pocket money to their children, they are telling them that they trust them and have faith in them, which boosts their self-esteem. They feel good and more confident about themselves.
3. When children start spending money to purchase things, they understand the value of money. They learn the important fact that their entire daily needs and other things need to be bought, for which they require money.
4. When children have to choose and decide how to spend their pocket money, it enhances their decision making skills, which are important life-skills.
5. When children learn to spend their pocket money in such a way that the expenditure is within the budget, they learn healthy judgment skills.
6. When children manage to meet their needs through their pocket money, they understand that money is a very important family resource and needs to be spent wisely.
7. Parents avoid power struggles on the demands of their children, because now the children are decision makers.
8. Parents save a lot of time, because children take care of their small needs with their pocket money, so that the parents can spend more quality time with them.

9. Children learn to say "No" to their own unreasonable demands, which teaches them the importance of regulating their wants and desires.
10. Children who are allowed to learn money management through pocket money are more likely to develop strong financial planning skills later on in their life.
11. When children are given pocket money, they feel that they are important members of the family because they have the power to spend family money.
12. Pocket money enables children to make choices. They also learn to wait for something for which they do not have money immediately but will have to save to acquire and possess it. So the children learn how to delay gratification.
13. Children can learn to manage money while they are still young and parents can guide them about it.

Money is an integral part of our day-to-day life and managing money is an important life-skill. Therefore, as parents, it is our responsibility to teach our children about managing money. We have to rise above our own fears and give an opportunity to our children to handle money. And the best tool to teach them money management is by giving them age-appropriate pocket money.

Stop Micromanaging My Life! Give Me a Break!

It was a typical Sunday when everybody was lazing around in the house. It was 11 in the morning and Seema was still sleeping. She was in Class 12 and her boards were round the corner. The environment of the house was full of pressure and anxiety about board exams. The only discussions that Seema's parents had the whole day were related to the board exams. Even when they were talking to their friends and relatives, their conversation always had a mention of board exams. Seema also had a younger brother who was in Class 9.

In the afternoon, the family was at the dining table to have lunch. Seema's Mom announced that she had taken a sabbatical for supporting Seema and taking care of her studies, so that she does not feel lonely, since she had immense pressure of her board exams. Seema couldn't say anything other than giving a faint smile. But in her heart she knew what it would be to have her Mom home.

By the last week of November, the regular school had almost come to an end. Seema had to stay at home for self-study. She had to go to school only for the second term exams and then for the pre-boards in January.

The ordeal had begun. Her Mom came into the room every morning and woke her up at 5.30 a.m. according to the study schedule they had made together. Her Mom had become a hostel warden in her own house. She had taken away Seema's mobile, which she would give to her only for an hour in the evening and when she went for tuition.

Seema's Mom was so anxious and insecure that she would not leave Seema alone even for half an hour so that Seema did not waste even a single minute. There was a fixed time for every activity. She was given her meals also by her Mom at a fixed time.

Seema felt as if she was a criminal and her house was a jail. Whenever she tried talking to her mother, she would be stopped. The only break Seema had was the time she spent going to the tuition centre. But from the time she left her home till the time she reached back, which was about two-and-a-half hours, there were at least 10 messages from her Mom, demanding each and every detail. Seema was so sick and tired of replying to the never ending questions of her Mom, that she had made standard answers and saved them. Whenever there was a question, she copied-pasted the answer and sent the reply by sms. The questions were irritatingly same and repetitive.

From the moment Seema entered her house, till the time she slept, her Mom would ask her, after every half an hour, what she would like to eat. Seema found a lot of solace in her washroom, but her Mom did not let her stay there for long. She would start knocking the door after 5 minutes.

Seema by now had an overdose of her Mom. The house started witnessing arguments between them every day. The moment her Mom tried to talk to her, Seema, unknowingly, snapped at her. Her Mom would wonder why this was so, after she had taken so much trouble and was trying to help her daughter. The situation took a turn for the worse when Seema's Mom overheard her daughter talking to her friend and saying, "I hate my Mom. She loves torturing me in the name of studies." Seema also told her friend that her Mom was not her real Mom but her Step Mom.

After hearing this conversation between her daughter and her friend, Seema's Mom could not control herself and burst into uncontrollable tears.

She could now only think of taking help from her friend, who was a counsellor. She really wanted to know where she had gone wrong. Her own biological daughter was accusing her with the label of a Step Mom, whereas she felt that since the time her kids came into her life, she had completely forgotten about her own self. She had sacrificed her outings, parties, pursuing her passion, to the extent that she took a sabbatical from her work, with a lot of difficulty, to be there with her daughter, to support her. And this is how her daughter felt about her! The words "hate" and "Step Mom" were stuck in her mind.

After a three hour long session with her counsellor friend, the feedback she got was an eye opener. She could not believe what she had done. The counsellor said that she, unintentionally, because of her own anxiety, had started micromanaging her daughter's life. Though she was trying to help, it was working the other way round. Her behaviour was very stifling and restrictive for Seema. The counsellor advised her to cancel her leave and immediately go back to work, so that she could also get a break from her home routines. Her daughter would also get a break from her constant nagging. The counsellor also advised her to get back to her normal, routine of life, because all her anxieties were getting conveyed to her daughter, who got an indirect message that she was not capable and responsible enough to manage her board exams herself.

Seema's Mom has joined her office back and Seema is feeling much better and relaxed. The environment at home is heading towards peace, finally.

Reflections

This story is one example of how we try to micromanage our child's life and how the child feels. There are many more examples around us, where parents over-indulge in parenting. Mothers, at times, get so involved that they get into a debate with the teachers if their child got even half a mark less than what they think he or she deserved. This causes a lot of embarrassment for a grown-up child.

I have seen mothers who want their children to become champions in whatever they do. There is this mother of a ten year old boy, who forces her child to go for swimming classes at 5 a.m. every day because she wants to make a champion out of him. There is another mother who forces her 15 year old child to go for karate classes early in the morning, when the child is so sleepy that he is hardly able to move his body.

We, the parents, forget that due to this attitude of ours, we are not only restricting the child's natural growth, we are also causing a hindrance to the mental growth and heading towards making our relationship with the child rough and sour.

As parents, it is our first priority to be involved in the task of parenting to help our children in their overall development. But it is also our responsibility to reflect on our parenting practices and see if we are suitably involved or over-involved or overindulgent. When we get over-involved, the whole process and experience becomes more damaging, instead of supporting and building the child.

Over-involvement in parenting is basically micromanaging, which is against the natural development of the child. We, as parents, need to empower our children and prepare them for life-skills rather than doing everything for them.

The micromanaging begins in the early formative years, when we start getting obsessed with what our child eats and get into unhealthy power struggles with our children. Then the next concern of ours is what the child will wear.

And this micromanaging goes on increasing when we start providing too much help in the homework and, at times, complete the project and the homework of our children for them. We forget that by these acts, we are not giving a chance to our children to become independent and feel confident about themselves.

Some of us try to invade the personal space of our children by expecting every little detail of every hour of the day from them. I would like to give an example of parents who till today book pizzas and order meals for their child who has gone to the US to study.

As parents, we all want to protect our children and want them to be safe and successful. But we can never accomplish this if we are always hovering over our children, always trying to control every little aspect of their life. Instead, we need to allow our children their own personal space, by letting them take decisions, face failures, face frustrations, face challenges, look for solutions, solve their problems on their own, and in the process become independent. We have to accept that we will not be there forever to hover over our children and protect them. And if our children have not become independent, it is probably the worst thing possible which we have done to them.

Because of all the micromanagement and our protective parenting style, our children might experience the following:

1. Develop an extremely low self-esteem. When we protect them and take all the control of their life in our hands, they feel they are not capable enough. They also feel that their parents don't trust them.

2. Develop extreme anxiety. Because of the over-interference of parents in their lives, children start experiencing high levels of anxieties. They become confused and can't take decisions. They become easily stressed out. The anxieties of parents also get passed on to the children.
3. Become "safe players" and avoid taking risks because they were never allowed by their parents to take risks. They were always warned and asked to play safe.
4. Children, over a period of time, become emotionally weak and have low tolerance for frustration and failures.
5. As a result of micromanaging, children become extremely dependent on others, like teachers in the class, and want to be assisted as much as possible.
6. The mental age of children might become lower than the chronological age. In spite of the fact that the children have high marks and grades, they might lack common sense, can never become street smart, and the overall maturity in these children gets delayed.
7. Their normal development gets hampered and individuals remain in the child mode. They can't grow into responsible adults who can handle their life, people, and situations, because their parents were constantly involved and never allowed them to face hardships and dangers and therefore never allowed them to grow. The children may also make statements like "I don't want to grow up."

The good news is that you can change these habits of yours by consciously withdrawing and giving space to your children. Mentioned on the next page are some strategies for you to step back and allow autonomy to your children.

1. Whenever you feel like going to your child's rescue, question yourself whether this act of yours will help the child become independent. If not, allow the child to handle the situation on his or her own.
2. Parents, you need to use the mobile phone, which is also known as the world's longest umbilical cord, judiciously. When parents want to get the status and position of their children every minute and hour, it is detrimental for the child's development. Instead, you need to encourage your children to take their own decisions and take responsibility of the results from the choices they make.
3. Practice and guide your children to become independent whenever they come to you asking for solutions. Instead of giving them instant solutions, you need to ask questions from them about how they would deal with the problem and what their idea of solving it is. When children are given opportunity to be independent, it promotes in them skills for self-regulation, persistence in the face of adversity, improvement in academic performance, and increases their sense of well-being.
4. As parents, it is very important to be consistent in your expectations from your children and let them face the consequences if they don't adhere to the rules, like withdrawal of privileges. This is because children need a boundary and a structure of rules.
5. Give yourself a break from parenting by having a sense of purpose, have hobbies to engage in, involve yourself with friends, and start spending "me time" with yourself.
6. Look at every problem as an opportunity to learn. Allow the children to brainstorm and explore options. Then you can deliberate on the feelings together and also talk about the consequences.

It is a very important duty to let our children think and act for themselves and take responsibility of the consequences of their actions. So, dear parents, let's give ourselves some reflective break time and let's try to move from being a micromanager to being a mentor and a guide to our children. Resist from the urge of jumping in and trying to fix everything for your child.

To sum up, I would like to say that babies require parents to micromanage for them because they are dependent and need constant attention for their holistic growth and development. But as they become older, we need to back off and keep giving them more and more space.

As adolescents, our children require support and guidance, as teenagers and young adults they require consultation and advice—only when they ask for it. When our children become adults themselves, they require freedom and partnership. We, as parents, need to keep tuning in to the wavelength of our children's developmental stage and accordingly indulge in parenting which will prepare them for the necessary life-skills.

I Was Adopted! The Shocking Truth

Mr and Mrs Seth lived happily with their two daughters till one day, in a family gathering, the other members suggested that they should try for another baby; maybe this time they would be blessed with a son. A son is a must, they said, to take the name of the family forward, because daughters get married and leave the house of the parents.

As they were already nearing 40, the Seths decided to adopt a son, instead. So they adopted a baby boy from an orphanage in Mumbai.

In no time this little boy became the centre of attraction for all the family members. Mr and Mrs Seth felt happy and proud of their decision to adopt a child.

With each passing day, their son Ayush started developing into an intelligent young boy. Meanwhile, their two biological daughters grew up into young ladies, who got married and moved away, into their own world. Now Ayush was the only one left with the Seths. He missed his sisters a lot.

After some time, it appeared that he had become very lazy. He started missing school and his grades also started falling. He was now in class 10, a critical year.

One day, while the family was at the dinner table, Ayush questioned his father. He asked, "Dad, my friends told me that I am adopted and not your biological child. Is this true?" The Seths were shocked, because they had been dreading the day this question would be asked. They had always felt insecure and confused as to how Ayush would react. Mr Seth patted him on his back and told him softly that he was their adopted child. Ayush pushed his chair, threw the plate from the dining table, and started screaming and crying.

That day was the darkest day for the family, because everything changed after that. Ayush locked himself in his room for more than 24 hours without food and water. He only came out of the room the next day, with many more awkward questions to ask.

He had a long list of questions and was looking for answers to all of them. Why did you adopt me, Dad? Where did you adopt me from? Why did my biological parents leave me? Give me the address of my biological parents — I want to meet them and ask them that why they abandoned me. Why was I rejected by them? These were some of the questions he asked.

Mr and Mrs Seth, patiently, tried to answer his questions, but not much could be achieved. From that day onwards, he started withdrawing himself from his friends, started missing school and felt very low and depressed. Some of his friends suggested to him that if he smoked a cigarette or two, he might feel better. Ayush wanted relief from his emotional tension and from that day he started smoking. Soon he was smoking about two packets a day.

Ayush felt very lonely because his family was not his own blood, though in fact they had done a favour to him by adopting him and giving him a life of comfort. He felt emotionally drained. With each passing day, his fights with his Mom increased. There were complaints from school regarding his performance in studies and behaviour. His health also started deteriorating.

On the suggestion of friends and relatives, finally, the Seths decided to meet an Adoption Counsellor. They are going for regular counselling sessions these days. Sometimes they accompany Ayush, sometimes they are called alone, and sometimes the counsellor calls Ayush alone.

Ayush is in class 11 now, and his parents are in the late 50s. Right now, the biggest achievement is that he has started opening up to this counsellor and has, at least started sharing how he feels about his adopted status.

For the Seths, he continues to be the apple of their eyes. They never ever had a thought, even for a single moment, that Ayush should be treated differently because he was adopted. Their only mistake was that they kept such an important fact hidden from him. He often taunts his mother that because he is not her biological son, she is ill-treating him, whereas the mother is simply being an involved parent.

Let's keep our fingers crossed, pray, and hope that the Seth's get their son back and peace can be restored in the family.

Reflections

There are many children who are deprived of their natural parents and a healthy environment for growth and development due to various circumstances and situations. Adoption is the best answer for this situation. So congratulations to all those parents who are practicing the sacred task of parenting through adoption.

The process of adoption is an intense, emotional experience for the adoptive parents. In the same manner, sharing the fact of adoption with the child is also a very sensitive experience. It usually causes a lot of anxiety in the adoptive parents, due to which they keep on postponing this sharing. This also happened in the case of Seths.

However, the story of adoption should start as soon as possible, when the child is around three years old and certainly before the child begins school. The word adoption should be used around the house with so much frequency that the child sees it as synonymous to being loved and wanted. In fact, the most appropriate and natural thing would be to give the child a big hug and kiss repeatedly and happily say, "We are so glad we adopted you." In this way the child will begin to associate the word "adoption" with feelings of love and a sense of belonging.

It is very important that the adoptive parents themselves explain the fact of adoption to their child rather than the child finding out from an outsider. For a child to learn about this emotional information from an outsider can be very traumatic, as it happened in the present case.

Informing the child about adoption is not a one-time affair. It is a gradual process, which needs to be handled over a period of time. Mentioned below are some workable tools which you can use when you talk to your child about adoption:

1. You can tell your child the story of his or her birth. You can begin by saying, "Some children are born into the family and some are chosen to be a part of it and you are our chosen baby."
2. You can also begin by sharing with the child, "For a long time, we wanted a baby just like you. We were lonely and our house seemed empty. Then a person told us about a place where there were babies and these babies wanted mummies and daddies. You were the baby we wanted, so we brought you home to be our very own forever."

3. Parents can also use the baby's photo album or a lifebook to explain the story of adoption.

When a child grows up knowing the essential facts of adoption, he or she is very comfortable with it at the later stages. However, the whole process has a very deep emotional meaning for both the parents and the child. For the welfare of the child, sharing the fact of adoption is an integral part of the adoption process and must be carried out at the appropriate age in the interest of the child.

11

I Got Carried Away

Malini was, as usual, working in her kitchen, when she got a call from her husband. What he said was extremely shocking. He said that he had got a call from a gentleman who said he was our well-wisher. He said that their son, Mohit, was into drugs; he smoked loaded cigarettes.

Malini almost fainted. She could not breathe and went numb. The first thought that came to her mind was, where did she and her husband go wrong? In spite of the fact that she had quit her high-paid government job to be with her children, how could her son get into something like this? Instead of they being aware of it, an outsider was giving them this feedback. How come?

Prabhat, Mohit's Dad, called up Malini again after some time and asked her if she was all right. He said that he had found that the person who had called was Mr Taneja, the father of Mohit's friend.

In the evening all of them were to meet at Mr Taneja's residence. Mohit's friend was also supposed to be there, so that the whole picture could become clear. When Prabhat had asked Mr Taneja how he came to know that Mohit smoked loaded cigarettes, he had said that his son, Roopesh, had told him. So he thought it was his moral responsibility to inform them.

When Prabhat came back from office in the evening, he and his wife discussed the whole matter. They tried to look at it from various angles. They were actively involved in the task of parenting. They had immense faith in their son. So they could not accept that their son was taking drugs. They strongly felt that there was more to the story.

When Mohit, who was in Class 11, came back from school and after he had rested well, his parents called him to the living room. Prabhat narrated the whole incident to Mohit and asked him what it was all about. He said, "Mohit, can you tell us how you know Roopesh? Why is he saying all this about you? What is the fact? Please share with us because, as far as we know you and the kind of values we have given you, this can't be true. But if there is any truth, then please tell us, because we really want to understand the whole picture before we actually meet Mr Taneja in the evening."

Mohit was also shocked. He told his Dad that he had met Roopesh at the coaching centre where he was taking classes for his engineering entrance exams. Roopesh was not from his school. He only knew Roopesh as an acquaintance. Since both of them lived in the same locality, they would often spend time together while travelling in the bus. They had no other interaction. Why his Dad was talking like this, he did not know. The fact that Roopesh had often shared was that his Dad was very strict and was a terror. To escape from the oppressive environment at home, Roopesh often drank alcohol and also smoked.

Now the pieces of the puzzle were falling in place for Mohit's parents. They could see the picture a little more clearly. But they wondered why Roopesh took Mohit's name.

Mohit and his parents reached Roopesh's house in the evening, as had been agreed. Mohit's Dad asked Roopesh, "Did you tell your Dad that Mohit is into drugs and takes loaded cigarettes?" Roopesh's answer was, "Yes." Then Mohit asked him, "When did you see me smoking cigarettes?

I hardly meet you anywhere other than the tuition centre." Roopesh replied, "I overheard you talking to your friends that you take loaded cigarettes and it is fun."

Mohit was shocked, but he had to come out with the truth. He said, "Children of our age find smoking very hip and look down upon those who do not smoke and drink. The other day, when you heard me, I was just bragging so that the other boys don't think I am a mamma's boy."

Roopesh had taken this bragging to be a fact. He shared it with his Dad when he had come late from his school's Conti party. He had earlier told his parents that he was going to his friend's home to study. His father came home early that day. When Roopesh returned late, his Dad saw that he was drunk. Roopesh's Dad could not control himself and started thrashing Roopesh. And when his Dad asked him why he was drunk, he had said, "Dad, I did not want to take, my friends forced me." And when his Dad asked him the name of his friends, he took Mohit's, along with two other boys. He thought that taking Mohit's name would be safe. His Dad would never be able to contact Mohit because he was not in his class. Roopesh was not in his senses at that time and was very scared.

But even in his wildest dreams, he did not imagine that this is how the situation will develop. Roopesh's father got the phone number of Mohit's father from the tuition centre which the boys attended and spoke to him. Roopesh acknowledged his mistake. He was ashamed and embarrassed about his act and apologized to Mohit and his parents.

Mohit's parents suggested the name of a counsellor for Roopesh. The meeting was fixed and what came out was an eye opener for Roopesh's parents.

The counsellor told them that Roopesh had started smoking and drinking at home because he had an easy access to both the things. His Dad was a chain smoker and had his quota of whisky every day. At times his Dad would ask his son to get him cigarettes from the store nearby. Sometimes he would ask his son to get some soda bottles or arrange for ice for his evening drink.

Since Roopesh was a teenager, there was an element of curiosity in him. His friends would often talk about how they enjoyed a drink and that it was so much fun once you were drunk. Smoking meant that you were grown-up and could handle your life yourself.

Hearing his friends talk about all this many times, Roopesh made up his mind to try drinking and smoking so that he could also boast about it. So one day, while he was alone at home since everybody had gone to attend a marriage, he opened his Dad's bar and made a drink for himself. He followed all the steps exactly like his Dad. First he poured the whisky in the peg measure and then into his glass. He added soda and some ice cubes. He had also stolen a cigarette from his Dad's cigarette pack. He took a sip of his drink, lit the cigarette and started smoking. He was emulating his Dad exactly. In doing all this, he felt great and big and all grown-up. He clicked a couple of selfies and posted them his Facebook page.

Thus began the story of substance abuse, all in his own house. Roopesh was smart enough to pour water in the bottle each time, to replace of whisky, so that his Dad could not find out.

Roopesh had a very strict father, who only interacted with him when there was a problem or when he got poor marks. His Dad would often hit him. Unwittingly, his Dad would also mistreat him emotionally when he would compare him with others and call him useless and fit for nothing. He would often blame his wife for spoiling Roopesh. Other than that, there was hardly any interaction between the two.

The drinking and smoking appeared to provide an escape to Roopesh from his regular problems. He started indulging

I Got Carried Away

in them regularly. Somewhere he was convinced that since his Dad also had them, it meant it was not so bad and when you become a grown-up, you could smoke and drink.

Roopesh was using drinking to hide his emotional anguish. He had also made friends who would often gather, in the name of group study, in a house where the family was out. Then they would go on a drinking and smoking binge.

At times, Roopesh's Mom suspected that he had smoked or was drunk, but she would ignore it. She knew that if Roopesh's Dad came to know of it, he would become very angry and the whole house would lose its peace. She was very scared of the anger attacks of her husband.

A typical evening in their house would be Roopesh in his room, his Mom in the kitchen and his Dad with his drink in the living room. Only three members in the entire house, but there was no interaction and no time ever spent together.

The counsellor suggested a detailed action plan which the parents had to follow with Roopesh. There were regular family therapy sessions, collectively as well as individually, before they could actually observe a positive change. Thankfully, now Roopesh is out of his habit. He is in the second year of an engineering college. Both the families have become close to each other and Mohit and Roopesh are best friends now.

Reflections

In the story mentioned above, Mohit and Roopesh were both very lucky that they could be saved from the dangers of substance abuse. Mohit's parents were keenly involved in the task of parenting and Roopesh's parents accidently discovered the problem. Recovery measures were taken, with suitable professional help from a counsellor. Roopesh recovered because he had a supporting friend and his family with him.

But everyone is not so lucky. Not all the parents are equipped with the tools to monitor the lives of their growing children. There are a lot of parents who are so busy in their personal and professional lives that they don't even know what their child is going through or what he or she is indulging in with friends. There are some parents who are aware that their child is getting addicted and into substance abuse, but have given up after trying once or twice. They have accepted that, actually, parents can just do nothing; nowadays all children indulge in substance abuse. There are some parents who go in a defensive shell, because whenever they try to correct their children, there are fights and arguments and the whole house is upset. A lot of mothers have started accepting the things the way they are. They hide the problems from their husbands because they are afraid that the peace of the house will be disrupted.

I am shocked and surprised every time I come across such parents who have given up on their children, saying they can't do anything about them. I feel like asking them that if you behave like this, what will happen to the child? Becoming a parent is a great responsibility. How can a parent ever give up on the child? If we focus on solutions, we will definitely find one suitable to us. But if we only look at the problems and condition our mind to believe that the times are bad, and we are helpless and can't do much about it, we will always remain stuck in the problem. We will never be able to help our children.

Have you ever wondered what will happen to the child if you give up? Parents, hope is something that we need throughout our lives. Make sure you have enough of hope, always. You will require this in abundance as parents.

Let us take a pledge that, as parents, we will not leave any stone unturned to prevent our children from getting into the clutches of substance abuse. For that to happen, we need to start and begin sensitizing them at home. Because home is the first institution of education, where all the teachings begin. The fact is that the family and parents are the most impactful teachers and leaders whom children love to imitate. Research shows that parents have a major impact on their child's decision not to use tobacco, alcohol, and drugs. This is because of the positive influence of the parents and because the children know it will disappoint them if they indulge in these things.

Parents can equip their children and prepare them to handle pressures and influences in school or college to get hooked on to substance abuse. This is why it is so important that parents build a strong relationship with their children by being aware, involved, and by talking to them about substance abuse.

We need to start as early as possible. By the time our children are four years old, they are well aware of the environment and are very curious and inquisitive. They are great observers. Mentioned below are some strategies which parents can practise at home to be able to prevent substance abuse, because prevention is always better than cure:

1. As parents, you are an influential role model for your children. You know your children better than anyone else. Only you can motivate them to think critically and make them understand the importance of valuing and respecting themselves and hence their bodies. They should be careful about what they put in their bodies. They should take good care of their physical, mental, and emotional health.

Family has an extremely important role to play in a child's life and, therefore, parents need to be the correct role models. Children observe how their parents and family members use alcohol, tobacco, and other drugs. The message they get is, if Mom and Dad are indulging into something, it means even I can follow them. Like it happened in the story of Roopesh, parents should never involve their children inappropriately, like asking them to fetch soda bottles or buy cigarettes for them.

Never drive your car when you are drunk. Get a driver for the time when you know you will be drinking or take a cab. It sends an extremely important message to children about safety and responsibility.

2. Early education is the key to prevention. Create platforms at home to talk to your children about substance abuse and its harmful impact on their brains and bodies. Equip yourself with the facts about alcohol, tobacco, and drugs before talking to them. Make time for regular conversations at home where you talk about how your children can be safe and talk about avoiding alcohol, tobacco, and drug use.

3. Develop clear, reasonable, and safe rules. Amend them as your child gets older. Some rules can be made in consultation with the child, but others should be non-negotiable. Be firm, have clear and consistent family rules, do not get influenced by what other families do. Your family rules show your family values. Discuss them in detail with your children and talk in advance about your expectations and the consequences for not following the rules. Encourage children to ask questions about anything that is not clear to them.

4. Intervene, address, and correct any wrong beliefs that your child might have, like when they say everyone smokes nowadays, everyone drinks, it is not possible to avoid passive smoking, and so on. Boldly bring up these topics and discuss and work towards changing the children's preconceived notions.
5. Keep your communication channels with your children always open. Talk to them by asking open ended questions. Listen to your children's concern non-judgmentally. Let them know you understand. Do not start preaching and correcting them immediately. If you do so, they might start avoiding you and might start shying away from conversation. Don't discuss or decide on consequences when either you or your child is angry or upset. Take a break to cool off and allow everyone time to reflect and gather their thoughts and then talk.
6. Talk to your child about being a leader or a follower. Listen to your child and let him or her know you understand the difficulties of coping with peer pressure. When your children are confident and secure, they will be better equipped to deal with the pressures of their peer group. Tell your children that when their friends ask them to do risky things, like use alcohol, tobacco, or drugs, it means they are not worth being your friends, so rejecting them is important. Peer pressure is an important determining factor for initiation of tobacco use among children and adolescents.
7. Role play and practise with your child how to say no to substance abuse when someone offers them these risky things. Tell them to repeat the slogan, "Say no to substance abuse and become a hero. Say yes to

substance abuse and you become a zero. And I choose to be a hero."

8. Be involved in your children's life, try and know their friends and their families and how your children spend time with their friends.
9. Tell your children, through your words and deeds, that they are your most prized possessions and that you value them and love them unconditionally. So it is also their duty to take good care of their physical, emotional, and mental health. They need to take good care of their own self and be safe. When you value your children, they value themselves. So gifting your child a high self-esteem is the best thing you can do as a parent.
10. Make sure to provide a platform to your children to explore their environment by motivating them to get involved in sports, pursue hobbies, join school clubs and activities, and so on.
11. Spend time together as a family. Look for activities that provide opportunities to spend time together.
12. Help your children to become good decision makers. Praise your children's strengths and accept them for what they are. Help your children to develop critical thinking skills like the ability to analyse and evaluate ideas, rather than simply accepting them as facts. Allow your children to practise decision making with an understanding of the consequences. Children need to learn how to make choices which are respectful, realistic, and responsible.
13. Show trust in your child, but also set boundaries. While children want to be independent, they also want limits placed on their freedom. But also show them how you, as parents, live with restrictions and boundaries.

Preventive checklist for parents to avoid substance abuse by their children

Q1. Am I a good role model?
Q2. Do I know how to communicate with my children?
Q3. Am I helping my children learn how to make responsible decisions?
Q4. Do I recognize that young people need increased independence?
Q5. Am I helping my children to cope with the pressures from their peer group?
Q6. Am I using positive disciplining techniques?
  Try to think, reflect, and find out the answers to these questions we have discussed.

Let us explore some probable causes why children get attracted to substance abuse

1. Because of curiosity, because they like experimenting, and because they want to experience how these things feel.
2. They are getting bored and want to relieve their boredom. So they indulge in these practices or seek out new risks.
3. Children think it is modern, smart, cool, and fun to be drinking and smoking.
4. Peer influence when they want to fit in the group.
5. Children who have an element of high risk-taking in their personality.
6. Children who want to get some relief from their stress and want relief from painful feelings mask their emotions and try to escape by using these things.
7. Children who have difficulty in dealing with feelings of aggression and derive excitement and pleasure out of being rebellious.

8. Children who have poor role models in parents.
9. Children who have negative, attention-seeking behaviour.
10. Children who have low self-esteem and are having learning difficulties.

How to initiate a talk on substance abuse with your children

To talk on substance abuse with your child, watch for opportunities which are natural and spontaneous. For example, you can initiate the talk after seeing something on a TV programme or news about substance abuse. Ask your children what they think about what they just saw and if they understand it.

Begin by acknowledging that people who are into substance abuse, do so for a reason. At least initially people get into substance abuse to satisfy their immediate need. Prescribed drugs are used to prevent disease, cure illness, or help in the normal functioning of the body. But people may also take drugs to change the way they feel, to feel good or happy, or to help them to forget and mask negative emotions, or simply in the name of relaxation. But when these drugs are used repeatedly, they increase the person's problems, rather than reducing them.

1. Ask open ended questions like, "Why do you think so many children are drinking and smoking these days?" rather than, "Have any of your friends asked you to smoke or drink?" The latter is a closed ended question and might make your child uncomfortable and defensive.
2. Try to avoid one-way communication, that is, lecturing. Have a two-way discussion where both of you listen to each other.

3. Keep a relaxed attitude and encourage your children to ask questions and tell you how they think and feel.
4. Be as concise and objective as possible when exploring the facts about substance abuse and discussing their pros and the cons.
5. Let your child know that you are talking to them about substance abuse out of concern for them, because you want to protect them, and because you love them. Show your willingness to trust their judgment.

Because parents are children's first role models they need to ask themselves:

"What type of an individual would I like my child to become?"

Write your answers, keeping in mind your inner characteristics, attitudes, and values. After writing the answer, read it and then ask yourself:

"Do I have these characteristics, values, and attitudes in me?"

As parents, are you willing to become the person who you want your child to be?

A life-skill activity for parents and their children

Tell your child about your experience when you were young and had to make a tough decision and were unsure of what to do. Make sure you share how you were feeling at that time about the matter, which was so challenging. Ask your child what he or she thinks you could have done or what he or she would have done in that situation.

The objective of the activity is to explore options, then have discussion on them. This is an activity that can be practised about any problem that the child and family may face. Exploring options is to recognize that there are choices in every situation.

To conclude, in order to protect and safeguard our children from substance abuse, we must make sure that the risk factors are reduced and the protective factors are increased. The guidelines of NIDA (National Institute of Drug abuse) are mentioned below for your reference.

Reduce the following risk factors

1. Ineffective parenting.
2. Chaotic home environment.
3. Lack of mutual attachment and nurturing.
4. Inappropriate behaviour in the class room.
5. Failure in school performance.
6. Poor social coping skills.
7. Affiliation with deviant peer group.
8. Perceptions of approval of drug using behaviours in the school, peer, and community environments.

Increase the following protective factors

1. Strong family bonds.
2. Parental monitoring.
3. Parental involvement.
4. Success in school performance.
5. Involvement of prosocial institutions (such as family, school, and religious organizations).
6. Conventional norms about drug use.

Bibliography

Bhattacharya, Soumya, *Dad's the Word: The Perils and Pleasures of Fatherhood*, Westland, 2012

Bonds of Love: Experiences in Adoption, Indian Association for Promotion of Adoption and Child Welfare, 1995

Chazot, Anju Musafir, Parenting Teens in Modern Times, Westland, 2013

Chona, Dr Shayama, *Effective Parenting*, Hay House Publishers(India) Pvt. Ltd., 2009

Chua, Amy, *Battle Hymn of the Tiger Mother*, Bloomsbury Publishing, 2011

Dadachanji, Dr Pervin, *Recipes for Parenting*, Rupa Co., 2006

Dange, Gouri, *More ABCs of Parenting*, Random House India, 2013

Dyer, Wayne W., *What Do You Really Want for Your Children?* Harper Collins Publishers, 1985

Faber, Adele and Elaine Mazlish, *How to Talk So Teens Will Listen & Listen So Teens Will Talk*, Piccadilly Press Ltd., 2005

Fedorschak Karuna, *Parenting: A Sacred Task*, Bhavana Books and Prints, 2004

Goleman Daniel, *Emotional Intelligence*, Bloomsburry Publishing, 1996

Harris, Thomas A., *I'm OK – You're OK*, Harper Collins, 2004

Jain, Hingad, Sugandha and Neera Jain, *Nurturing Emotional Intelligence*, Scholars Hub, 2008

Kale, Smita, *Understanding Indian Teens*, WMI Books

Karwa, Payal Shah, *The Bad Touch*, Hay House Publishers (India) Pvt. Ltd., 2014

Kenny, Cedric M., *Love Without Spoiling*, Discipline Without Nagging, Wisdom Tree, 2004

Mehta, Nilima, *Ours by Choice: Parenting through Adoption*, Indian Association for Promotion of Adoption and Child Welfare, 1992

Prasad, Gitanjali, *The Great Indian Family*, Penguin Books Ltd., 2006

Rudolph, Steven, *Solving the Ice-Cream Dilemma*, Bennett Coleman & Co. Ltd., 2011

Sanyal, Smita Barooah, *Understanding Addictions*, Roli Books Pvt. Ltd., 2012

Singh; Chayanika, *How Your Personality Makes or Breaks Your Child: A Self-Assesment Guide for Parents*, Unicorn Books, 2013.

Templar, Richard, *The Rules of Parenting*, Pearson Power, 2008

The Yellow Book: *A Parent's Guide to Sexuality Education*, Tarshi, Zubaan, 2010

Trehan, B. K. and Indu Trehan, *Building Great Relationships*, Sterling Publishers (P) Ltd., 2010

• • •